ADVANCE PRAISE

Defying Death on the Danube is an amazingly detailed story of a SURVIVOR!! Horst (Henry) Stern. Incredible! I am so thankful his story is being told. We watch movies and documentaries of men and women who have endured horrifying circumstances and have fought to survive in life. Henry's story gave me such a beautiful inside perspective of a life that started off with similar challenges that we as humans face such as parental failures, children being moved to Grandparents/family members, financial struggles - all things that we may be able to relate to. However, this story moves very quickly to events that are so difficult to even comprehend! The Holocaust was beyond human "normalcies". Henry's story is so real. Just to have a firsthand account in such details of this man's day to day life is remarkable! I thoroughly enjoyed it from start to finish. I found myself rushing through parts to get to the end of that paragraph or page to see what happened. I love the author's writing style. She brings out the humanness of Henry and his family. I could feel Henry's sense of humor as he talked with Mrs. Callahan. I could feel the powerful bond that Henry, his Mom and Grandmother had from start to finish, even with the barrier between Henry and his Mom due to the "unknown" Dad. As I read of Henry's many escapes and moments of good-luck, I just knew he had to have an Angel helping him along the way. Another highlight I want to make is when Selma recited the poem she had memorized from her childhood and how emotionally overwhelming it was. So beautiful! I appreciate that Mr. Stern was willing to be transparent and vulnerable to the world. It is also astounding that Henry remembered this incredible story in such detail. Amazing! Debbie has written this book with such honor and respect for the family and all Holocaust survivors. - **Sandra Renkel**

"War is Hell," General William Tecumseh Sherman. This was a major understatement. The real hell reveals itself when the shooting ceases. It is the turmoil and conflict which has seeped so far into the crevasses of the victims' souls and hearts that it will never be completely purged.

Horst Stern was raised in the shadows of poverty that covered most of Germany post-World War I. Though basic necessities were scarce his family was able to scrape by. Then came the Nazi regime and their sinister scheme to annihilate all Jews and Jewish sympathizers. Survival instincts were the only way to escape certain death. Scrounging for food became a daily occurrence, not food that most would consider edible, rather any substance that would fill the stomach. This is a psychological journey that paints the depth of which a man will go to survive.

The story outlines Horst Stern's journey through life and how he continues to push the scars of the war out of his life. It's a testament to his courage to not only survive but thrive. Though he admits to many times having a hollow feeling, he continues to seek ways to rise above. With his determination and persistence, he made a better life for his mother, grandmother, and self.

It speaks to me about all the victims of war, not just the obvious one, such as the Stern family. When I was living in Tampa in the late 70s, the company I worked for did business with a German machinist, who lived through World War ll. He related to me how wonderful Hitler was. That he was good for Germany. He acknowledged the concentration camps and felt the Jews needed to be sent there. The man was a victim of hatred that undeniably altered his destiny.

I knew another man in the 1980s, who was a pilot for the Luftwaffe. At one point his plane was shot down and was a prisoner of the Allied Forces. Whereas he didn't believe Hitler was right, he denied that there was a massacre of the Jews. The man was a victim of psychology denial, which undoubtedly ruled his life in many areas.

After the war, Horst has met people like these two men, further reminding him of what personal torture he went through.

Debbie Callahan has masterfully retold Horst's story. Through his eyes we are able to smell, taste and feel all trials he endured. The unprovoked persecution an entire group of people suffered. The rage and aguish he felt pour from the pages. Thankfully, so does the hope and determination. In the end this is a story of triumph. In order to make it a total victory we must read and understand the perils of hatred. We must be the shield that protects our world from a repeat of this tragedy. - **John Klopfer**

In *Defying Death on the Danube*, Debbie Callahan gives readers a glimpse of the meaning of survival. Although the subject is one of sadness toward the inhumanity of mankind, the story is wonderful and light. As the readers follow Henry's journey through life, they can easily visualize the places, experiences, and, most importantly, the personal connections. Callahan used Henry's story and words as a foundation for this masterpiece and then infused it with her own emotions. Overall an unforgettable read. - **Liz Thompson**

DEFYING DEATH ON THE DANUBE

A HOLOCAUST SURVIVAL STORY

DEBBIE J CALLAHAN

HENRY STERN

ISBN 9789493231429 (ebook)

ISBN 9789493231412 (paperback)

ISBN 9789493231436 (hardcover)

Publisher: Amsterdam Publishers, The Netherlands

info@amsterdampublishers.com

Defying Death on the Danube is part of the series Holocaust Survivor True Stories

Copyright © Debbie J. Callahan, 2021

Cover picture: Budapest (Public Domain via Creative Commons)

All Rights Reserved. No part of this publication may be reproduced or transmitted in any form or by any means, electronic or mechanical, including photocopy, recording or any other information storage and retrieval system, without prior permission in writing from the publisher.

CONTENTS

Prologue	1
Acknowledgments	5
1. Berlin	7
2. Times of Change	14
3. Budapest	20
4. School Days	28
5. Becoming a Man	31
6. Forced Labor	35
7. The March	42
8. The Budapest Ghetto	58
9. The Russians are Coming	69
10. The Aftermath	74
11. Barter and Trade	78
12. The New Beginning	85
13. A New Career	90
14. Vienna	95
15. Saving Selma	99
16. Life in a DP Camp	108
17. Waiting for Immigration	114
18. Everyone Loves a Man in Uniform	126
19. Israel	134
20. The Reunion	149
21. Goodbye Ladies	156
22. Back to Europe	160
23. Oh Canada!	165
24. Toronto	175
25. St. Croix	185
26. The Well Deserved Extended Vacation	209
27. Going to America 1988	214
Afterword	219
Photographs	225
About the Author	229
Amsterdam Publishers Holocaust Library	231

When Henry originally wrote his own story, he poured hours and years into working on his manuscript for only one reason. He wanted future generations to realize the heinous acts that have been, and might be again, committed in the name of hatred. His goal was that others might learn from his experiences. For that tireless effort, I'm eternally grateful.

I dedicate this retelling of his story to him, Horst (Henry) Stern. Not only did he survive atrocities most of us can only imagine, but also as a teenager, he stepped up and protected his mother and grandmother throughout the war.

Courageously, he shared his Holocaust survival story, but instead of dwelling on being a victim, he has used writing, art, and humor as a means to cope with the past. He is a true hero, and I'm honored that he has trusted me to keep his story alive.

Debbie J. Callahan

PROLOGUE

Following my locally publicized trip to Auschwitz for the 70th Anniversary of the liberation, the mayor of my city, a man I had never met, contacted me. We met, and he requested my assistance in putting together the Holocaust Remembrance event for the city. Immediately, I knew that I wanted to find some Holocaust survivors to participate in a candle lighting ceremony during the event. I needed assistance finding some, and through a local rabbi, I came across Henry Stern.

I have a great amount of respect for Holocaust survivors and I'm in awe of the situations that they had the strength and courage to withstand. To this day, even with as many as I have met and as often as I have talked to them, I'm still apprehensive to make initial contact. I never know what to expect. Some are wonderfully receptive, some too wracked with painful memories and frequent nightmares to discuss much of anything, and I have to respect whichever reaction I receive. Henry's response was by far one of the most interesting I had ever received. His light humor was immediately evident as he spoke in riddles that not only made me laugh, but also made me think and reflect. At once, he agreed to participate.

Early on in our correspondence, I asked him if he could send me a little information about himself that I could use in a short biography, to be read as he approached the ceremonial table to light his candle at the Holocaust Remembrance event. His email reply included a 315-page copy of the manuscript he had written. I downsized it to about five main points that could be used for his introduction, a monumental task. At that time, I couldn't have known how much more time I would spend with Henry's written work.

At the ceremony, I gave each survivor a copy of a book I had written about Holocaust survivors. Shortly after the ceremony, Henry asked if I would be interested in writing his story and invited me to his home to discuss it. Within two weeks, I called on the Sterns.

Visiting Henry's home showed me that the creativity of his writing and speaking didn't stop there. He clearly has an artistic soul. The home he shares with his lovely wife, Barbara, is adorned with his paintings and sculptures he created from rare woods. A quick walk down the hallway of their modest mobile home led to his studio. There, surrounded by paintings, painted handmade jewelry, and supplies, I caught a glimpse of the way his mind works. Nothing is trash and nothing is wasted, he paints on broken CD discs, used medicine cases, and Plexiglas, turning trash into treasure. He doesn't consider himself an artist and has no idea if his work will ever be worth anything to anyone other than himself; yet, he continues to pour hours into it.

Perhaps his artwork is evidence of releasing all the turmoil that undoubtedly occupies a great deal of real estate in the mind of any Holocaust survivor. I suppose it is his escape, but that is a personal assumption. He sent me home with several of his paintings, pieces of his unique jewelry, and he let me choose a wooden sculpture. As he handed the treasures over to me, he said that if ever any of his work was to sell, he wants the proceeds to go to The United States Holocaust Memorial Museum.

As honored as I was when he bestowed pieces of his art on me, I felt even more so when he chose to leave his story in my hands. Handing me an old copier box filled with the typed manuscript of a book he had previously published, other articles that he had written since, hand-written notes and manuscript pages, and some pictures, he asked me to do something with it. The handwritten manuscript itself was a treasure, but reading Henry's notes helped me learn so much more about him. His notes were on everything from current affairs to pages upon pages of conversations that he had with God. Fascinating!

His book, *Horst: The Misadventures of a Holocaust Survivor*[1], was told honestly and effectively in his own voice, in his broken English, and in it, the reader can see his blunt descriptions and humor. Yet, he asked me to retell his story in my own way and in a reader-friendly manner, saying that he wanted only to share the "Never forget! Never again!" message. "I tried telling it my way; it's your baby now." I knew only that I still wanted this to be his story and for the reader to see his character, but I also knew that I needed to show the severity of what Henry experienced.

Here, I hope to show what one boy, and his family, suffered in the name of hatred. I hope you will see what human beings are capable of doing to one another when racist, antisemitic, anti- any particular religion, or other hate-based attitudes are allowed to go unchecked.

Here is Henry's story, rewritten at his request, but with much of his own writing intertwined from his book, *Horst: The Misadventures of a Holocaust Survivor*, his notes, and other writings.

---

1. Stern, Henry, *Horst: The Misadventures of a Holocaust Survivor*, Publish America, June 2006.

ACKNOWLEDGMENTS

This project has been years in the making, and although it is a mixture of my words along with those of Henry Stern, there are so many more people beyond the two of us who have played a part and who deserve acknowledgement.

Always by Henry's side is his lovely wife Barbara. She welcomed me so graciously into their home and fully supported my retelling Henry's story when he asked me to rewrite it for him, a story in which she has been an important part. Just as Henry trusted me in handing over all of his writing, so too did she place her trust in me, for which I'm grateful.

As I worked to piece this book together, my own husband, Scott Sepper, supported me by accepting and understanding the time I devoted to it and encouraged me to continue during difficult times. It wasn't always easy to tell someone else's story, definitely not as easy as telling my own in my own voice, but when the frustration set it, Scott would remind me of the importance of the project, and my focus would soon return. I appreciate him so much.

My friends and family have always supported my writing, but there is one friend in particular whom I would like to recognize here. Simon Bell understands both the work and emotions involved in working with and writing about Holocaust survivors. As an author of Holocaust-related books himself, he knows that they are a rare breed and feels the same sense of awe and humbleness at having their trust and being able to share their stories. I'm grateful for our many discussions, sharing of book titles and other resources for research, and for his willingness to help me stay motivated.

Admittedly, I'm a Facebook junkie, and it was on that social media platform that I discovered a page called Buildings Tell Tales. If there was anything I could have done differently before completing this book, it would have been to actually travel to Budapest to walk in Henry's footsteps. With that not being possible, this Facebook page was definitely the next best thing.

Finally, I'm forever grateful to Liesbeth Heenk and Amsterdam Publishers. When looking for a publisher for this book, I wanted to go in a different direction than I had with those I had previously written. I was impressed at the focus that Amsterdam Publishers had on Holocaust memoirs and felt like it was the perfect fit for Henry's story. Once I met with Liesbeth, via Zoom, I felt instantly comfortable with her and knew that she could help bring this story to life. Upon reading it, she accepted the book for publication, and offered great advice on more than one occasion to help me make the changes necessary to create the finished product you see today. I can't thank her enough for taking a chance on this book.

1

BERLIN

Nice Jewish girls didn't have affairs with married men in 1928 Berlin and especially with men not of their faith. This couldn't happen without a price to pay, without becoming the family outcast. The indiscretion sealed Erna's fate as the family's black sheep. Into this chaos, Horst Stern was born, and his distressing entry into the world was an ominous foreshadowing of events to come.

Erna hid her secrets well and eventually even took some to her grave. She wouldn't even admit that she was aware of her pregnancy. From the day she brought disgrace to their door to the day her parents threw her out of it, she refused to divulge the name of Horst's father, but later it became known that he was her boss at the time of the affair.

Erna's mistake not only impacted her parents. She was the youngest of three children born to Izsak and Selma Stern. Her brother Robert, born May 28, 1902, preceded her by four years, and her sister Rosa, born in 1900, by six years. There was also extended family. Prior to World War II, the Stern clan was a vast one but much of it was decimated by Hitler's Nazis, and it's safe to say, Erna's indiscretion certainly created a stir throughout the entire group.

Exactly where and what the circumstances were during these

early years of Horst's life in Berlin will forever remain a mystery. He knows nothing of his time alone with Erna, but eventually, his mother deposited him at the home of his grandparents on Kant Strasse 69, Charlottenburg, and walked out of his life.

Both of Horst's grandparents were over 60 years old, and another child was the last thing they expected after having long since raised their own three children. However, they adapted, because it was left to them to raise young Horst, and they did so, on and off, for the next nine years.

Selma Stern was the anchor in Horst's life, and despite her earlier disappointment in her daughter's poor choices, she stepped in and became everything her grandson needed.

From left to right: Selma Stern, Horst Stern, Erna Stern. Photos: Arolsen Archives

Describing her as a four foot eight inch giant, he credits her with shaping his life and giving him the foundation on which he was able to build his values. Born in 1866 in Berlin, Selma lived to the age of 87, she died of natural causes in Canada. She was the only one of her five sisters and two brothers to have the luxury of dying in such a natural manner. Horst loved and cared for his grandmother dearly until the day she died.

Once, Horst asked his grandmother if she knew who his father was, and she said that she did, explaining that when Horst was still an infant, his biological father showed up one day and tried to claim him. She refused to give up her only grandson to a stranger, though. He sometimes tried to picture what would have happened to him if his grandmother had let him go. Thoughts of how he might have been brought up by his non-Jewish German father have kept him eternally grateful that his grandmother refused to hand him over to his biological father. Unwanted visions of uniforms and forced drills as a recruit of the Hitler Youth infiltrated his dreams, but he shook them off knowing that Selma would never release him to the stranger whose blood he carried.

Izsak Stern, Horst's grandfather, was born in Budapest, Hungary, in 1870. Prior to the First World War, he used to make a very good living as a cigar salesman. During the war, he served in the Hungarian Army, but once it ended, he was never able to get back on his feet. It wasn't for lack of trying. In an effort to support his family, Izsak sold high quality cigars for a time, but he also smoked them to the point that he eventually developed tuberculosis. He succumbed to it in 1940. Horst remembers him with fondness, but adds that, "he scared the living hell out of me for years."

Too young to remember the actual move, Horst does recall the family moving not too far away to Knesenebeck Street 76 when he was three years old. The fact he remembers the address to this day still surprises him, "Some people I met yesterday who gave me their names, I don't remember." He describes an apartment just like thousands of others in Berlin. Situated in the rear on the third floor, their apartment consisted of three bedrooms, a big kitchen, and a long hallway leading to the bedrooms. There was also the *die gute Stube*, German for the living room or parlor, which was only used for birthdays, holidays, or when one of the family members visited.

Horst and his uncle, Robert, shared one bedroom with a big double bed. His grandparents occupied the second bedroom, and the third one was usually rented to a single man, the income from which was much needed for the struggling Stern family.

At the age of four, Horst was able to enroll in the Jewish kindergarten in the neighborhood where he spent the next two years learning how to get along with the rest of the world. Selma dropped him off there at around seven each morning picked him up at five in the afternoon.

Six was the magical age when children were able to begin *Kinderhort*, and Horst was among them. Students attended it until they finished elementary school at the age of 14. Normally, when students graduated from elementary school, they either went to a trade school, which lasted another four years, followed by two more years if they wanted to become a master in a profession, or they took the high school and college route.

When he started school in 1934, Horst's routine changed. He walked to school by himself, which was about a mile, and after that, hiked to the Kinderhort. Once he arrived there each day, he had lunch, followed by 30 minutes of relaxation. Then he did homework and once completed, if there was time left, he played games with his friends until it was time to go home. Until he was eight years old, his grandmother used to pick him up, but after that, he was on his own. Considering his early beginning and absent parents, his childhood was much like that of any other young German boy.

Once, when he was still quite young and following his ordinary route, something quite extraordinary caught his attention. He and his friend Itzack came across a Nazi rally with tens of thousands of people lining the streets. Swastika flags flew from every pole. The frenzied atmosphere was electrified with people anxiously anticipating the chance to glimpse the Führer pass by. The two small and agile boys were able to squeeze through the throng of people and get right up to the front row just in time for the one of the most unforgettable moments of Horst's life.

Thousands of onlookers yelled the familiar, *"SIEG HEIL"* (Hail to the Führer). The two naive youths couldn't resist getting caught up in the jubilation and soon began to salute and chant as well, because although they were Jewish, they were first and foremost, Germans, and didn't realize any threat to their way of life. Shortly after, Hitler walked by them as they stood with their right hands stretched out in the Hitler salute. The Führer passed barely ten feet from them. When he thinks back on this event now, he realizes that it was kind of interesting to be part of history and to witness what turned out to be evil personified to the highest degree.

Adolf Hitler - Photo: Public Domain

Throughout the years spent at kindergarten, Horst was never made to realize that there was something wrong with his speech. In regular school; however, one of his teachers recognized that he needed the assistance of a speech therapist. He had often been told by his grandmother, and the staff at the kindergarten to slow down when he spoke, but he never considered it a problem.

In his mind, he was just a kid who spoke too fast, and in doing so, jumbled his words. He also realized that he had trouble with words that started with a K or G, and the result was that he stuttered. The severity of the problem became apparent when he entered elementary school, and it was a challenge that he faced throughout the remainder of his time in school. At that time, there was no way of knowing that bigger obstacles were still to come.

When Horst was no more than seven or eight years old, he was playing with some friends at school, when one of the *Tantes* (females who worked at the Kindergartenhort) in charge approached him and told him to follow her because there was a lady waiting to meet him. Filled with dread, he reluctantly followed wondering what he did wrong this time.

Unable to recall any recent misdeeds, he continued to follow the Tante into the next room, which was empty except for an elegantly dressed, tall lady who stood there, with her petite hat and a fox fur wrapped around her neck. Horst recalls the fox's head biting its tail, looking at him with his two big glass eyes. The Tante called him over and introduced him to the lady, "Horst, this lady is your mother." All Horst could come up with was, "Did you bring me something?"

While looking into Horst's eyes, his mother said, "Don't you remember me?" She held out her hands, but Horst just looked at the Tante and asked her if he could go back and play. He wouldn't see Erna again until 1940. The meeting left little impact on Horst, and life with his grandparents continued to move forward, although not without struggle.

Iszak Stern's illness made it difficult for him to work, but he tried to eke out a living by parking at a corner by Olivaer Platz and selling toiletries, cosmetics, and other items from a pushcart. Conditions were anything but ideal for his grandfather's health, especially in wintertime.

Iszak's frequent coughing frightened young Horst. Many evenings, his grandmother went over to her sister's house, about a ten-minute walk away, to play cards with her and some other ladies. It seemed to Horst his grandfather's coughing spells were worse in the evening than during the day, and he remembers that when they came on, it was usually so severe that in order to drown out the sound of the coughing, he would start singing at the top of his voice while marching around the dining room table, but one night, when Horst was eight years old, his grandfather's suffering particularly concerned him.

Already in his nightshirt one night in the middle of winter, Horst was home alone with his grandfather when he heard him coughing quite hard. From sheer worry, without even thinking, he ran bare foot down the stairs and onto the snowy street in an attempt to find the house where his grandmother was and tell her that his grandfather was dying. Before he could reach the house though, he was stopped by a policeman. After asking where he was running to, bare foot, in the middle of the night, he took Horst back home. His grandfather never realized Horst was gone.

While Iszak's coughing was a constant concern for Horst, he was used to his grandfather's illness. He had never known anything different. The majority of the responsibility for his care fell on his grandmother's shoulders, and even at his young age, he appreciated and respected Selma for the vital role she played in his life.

In addition to taking care of her family, Selma Stern worked at home at her Singer foot pedal-operated sewing machine. She created aprons for butchers and other tradesmen from patterns she cut out from rubberized material.

Horst's Uncle, Robert, also contributed money toward the rent and food. With Iszak's illness, Robert stepped in and acted as father figure to young Horst. He was the only person who ever spanked him, at Selma's insistence. Usually, all it took to keep Horst's behavior in line was the threat of reporting his behavior to Uncle Robert. Spankings were rare, but when they occurred, it was Horst's dignity more than anything else that was hurt, and admittedly, it deterred future misbehavior, for a little while anyway.

Horst loved his uncle, deeply. However, the time came when Robert met a Polish-Jewish woman, Fela (Felicia), and began a relationship with her, marking the beginning of the end of Horst's close relationship with his uncle. Following a very short courtship, Robert Stern married Felicia and moved out of the house, and in doing so, instantly changed young Horst's life. When Horst met his new aunt for the first time, he remembers it was "hate at first sight," and he wondered what he had done to push Uncle Robert away from him.

At nine years old, feeling deserted, he blamed himself. Guilt enveloped Horst because he realized that all of his trouble at school just might have pushed Robert away. Perhaps, Robert had to deal with Horst's misbehavior at school one too many times. Yet, he just couldn't seem to stay out of trouble.

2

TIMES OF CHANGE

Although he didn't think it possible, after Robert's departure, Horst's stuttering got worse, as evidenced during an assignment from the teacher to learn a poem that he had to recite within a few days. Although he studied for hours, until he was sure he had it right, when the teacher called his name out to recite it, he stood up, and even though he knew the whole poem in his mind, all that came out of his mouth was something like, "Mmmary had a lllittle lllllamb." Almost immediately, the other students burst out laughing. Horst just stood there and eventually spoke up only to call everyone in the class, "Ssshit-ffface." That only served to make things worse. His classmates began laughing so hard that all he could do was sit down, he didn't speak for the rest of that day. His speech impediment and the reaction of his classmates contributed to his behavioral problems in school.

Not a week went by when Selma wasn't called into school to talk to the principal about her grandson's behavior, about his not fitting in with the other children, fighting with them, and his often-disruptive behavior. Despite his behavioral issues, he studied hard in the beginning, but when he was called upon to answer a question aloud, he froze up and eventually just stopped trying and wouldn't speak.

Teachers and family urged Horst to speak slowly, but when he tried he felt that he only "ended up stuttering in slow motion," as he referred to it. In the end, it took another country and another language to semi-cure his speech impediment.

Horst's speech impediment didn't seem to hinder his performance in math and sports, in which he earned A-plus ratings, but his first two years at school weren't easy for him. He honestly doesn't know how he passed but suspects that it was easier for the teachers to promote him so that the next teacher would have to deal with him. His luck ended during his third year of school when a teacher, with a better understanding of his stuttering problem, felt the need to have him repeat the grade.

Despite the many hardships in his life, Horst had a few unique opportunities. In the summer of 1937, the Berlin-Jewish-Organization put together a transport for children of low-income families for a two- or three-week vacation to Sweden. Horst was among the children selected to go. They stayed in a place called Cristinchoo, and the house itself was known as Vastrabygard. He recalls the trip:

"Getting there was really an adventure itself. First we went by train, and that same train went onto a ship, which sailed for some time till it got to a place in Sweden where the train just continued to move back onto the rails, and tallyho, on we went till we got to the place called Cristinchoo." (Stern, 2006)

The next three weeks were like being in heaven for Horst. Never had he eaten so well or so much, and he put on about five pounds to show for it. All too soon, it was time for his respite to end, and for him to return home to Berlin, a city that quickly became more threatening for the young boy. There were many days when only his athletic ability saved him from getting a beating by members of the *Hitlerjugend* (Hitler Youth). These were Nazi-trained boys who frequented the Jewish neighborhood looking for Jewish kids to beat up. The odds were usually in their favor, four-to-one. Horst knew the neighborhood well enough to run away from them, but he occasionally got caught, which resulted in a few tears and bruises.

Finally, realizing that they were all in danger in Germany with

Adolf Hitler in charge, Horst's grandparents started making plans to leave. Since his grandfather had been born in Hungary and was able to keep his citizenship, he could easily return there. He did so in 1937, and his grandmother planned to follow within the next year.

Meanwhile, the excitement in Berlin escalated and took a turn for the worse, as Horst witnessed first-hand one day. While walking to school on the morning of November 10, 1938, he was shocked to see that all the storefront windows had been smashed. Masses of people were looting the Jewish stores, while the police looked on. Not only were they doing nothing to stop the violent acts, but they actually encouraged the looters.

Kristallnacht. Photo: Public Domain

Even at his young age, Horst couldn't believe what he heard coming from the very people who were supposed to protect them. "Take what you want. Those stinking Jews are going on a one-way trip on a permanent vacation." None of the gentiles who witnessed this happening made a comment. A few just shook their heads; the rest laughed and joined in the looting. Nothing made sense to Horst anymore.

Frightened and confused, he maneuvered the glass-covered sidewalks in the area of Charlottenburg, Fasahnen Strasse in Berlin. Horst looked up, and in the distance, saw his school. Smoke rose to the sky, but curiosity outweighed his fear and compelled him to continue on in that direction. Along the way, he encountered some kids returning from the school who immediately informed him that their school and synagogue had been torched by the Nazis. Later, he learned that incidents like this had taken place all over Berlin.

Left: Kristallnacht. Photo: German Federal Archive (Wikipedia Commons). Right: Interior of the Fasanenstrasse Synagogue, destroyed during Kristallnacht. Photo: Public Domain

Young Horst had just witnessed the result of *Kristallnacht* (The Night of Broken Glass) or Crystal Night, which was a government-sanctioned pogrom (riot) that took place in many cities across Germany and in other locations in Europe, from November 9 to 10 in 1938. It was an unforgettable night that effectively ended Horst's formal schooling at that particular school.

Surprisingly, some of the Jewish schools survived, and Horst was sent to one located in a different district of Berlin, about three to four kilometers from where he lived. It took him over an hour to get there. Since his family couldn't afford it, a streetcar wasn't an option. As he worked to fit in at the new school, students began to disappear. Without explanation, there would be fewer and fewer classmates each day, and those who vanished were never seen or heard from again. Remaining students had no idea what happened until much later when they learned that their former classmates got picked up by the Nazis and were sent to various concentration camps.

Once again, the remaining students were sent to the last remaining Jewish school, which he believed, was the one located on Klopstock Strasse, Berlin. It may have been the Jewish Zionist School that was in operation on that street until 1939. Schools continued to close one at a time, and people he knew continued to disappear. Some left because they had the money to escape Germany, which wasn't easy or cheap, but at that point, it was still possible for those with wealth and the right connections.

Later, Horst realized that those who couldn't afford to leave, or who were still under the delusion that nothing bad would happen to loyal, good, upstanding German citizens, stayed and took their chances. They in no way thought that they would be targeted. This false sense of security would end up costing hundreds of thousands of people their lives. Eventually, that myth was shattered, and the majority of them never made it back. Most of them perished in various ways at one of thousands of labor camps, concentration camps, or extermination camps.

One day, during the midst of all of these disappearances, Horst found out that the Jewish Organization in Berlin was putting together a transport of children to be sent to Australia. Although this might have spared him the danger of life as a Jewish boy in Berlin, and he qualified, his grandmother refused to let him go. In his young mind, that proved to him that he must have done something right or wasn't as bad as he had thought. Eventually though, Horst's grandmother joined her husband in Hungary, and once again displaced, Horst moved in with Uncle Robert and his new wife, Felicia, in Berlin.

Moving into his uncle's home was uncomfortable for Horst because he still didn't like his new aunt, but there was no other option. Her insistence on forcing him to do things he never had to do before, such as washing his own clothes, did little to alleviate his dislike for her. Under her guardianship, he even had to learn how to darn his socks and do occasional ironing of socks, handkerchiefs, and his own shirts, all of which he resented. He suddenly had to sit straight at the dining table, and he was shown how to hold a fork and knife correctly, but the young boy especially hated that he had to take a bath every day. Certainly, this would make anyone seem evil in the eyes of a ten year old boy.

Robert's wife's philosophy, as far as eating was concerned, was, "No one can look into your stomach, but everyone will judge you by how you look." Concerned with appearances, Felicia didn't want the three of them to appear malnourished. At dinner each night, she made Horst drink two glasses of water before eating, because it would miraculously diminish his hunger and he ate so much less.

Unintentionally, all of the skills Felicia taught Horst came in handy during the hardships he was soon to face. In realizing that, he eventually found a new appreciation for his aunt, and felt guilty for the mean things he had often said about her behind her back. The last time he saw her was in Tel Aviv in 1949, a few years after the murder of her husband, his beloved Uncle Robert, at the hands of the Nazis at Auschwitz Concentration Camp.

3

BUDAPEST

Violence and restrictions progressively worsened for the few Jews who remained in Berlin over the next two years. Yet, despite living in constant fear, there were still the few holdouts who stayed because they felt they would be spared. Although they had lost their rights to citizenship, they stayed loyal to their country even if they couldn't support the government. After all, some of them had fought for Germany during the First World War and had the wounds and medals for bravery and loyalty to prove it. They couldn't imagine all of that would be forgotten, and their lives would be endangered as the enemy now. As far as the new German Reich was concerned, none of that mattered. There was only one good Jew, and that was a dead one. Any who might have felt safe existed under a false sense of security.

What had at first begun as rules of inconvenience, such as being forbidden to be outdoors after 8 p.m. in winter, 9 p.m. in summer and the confiscation of their wireless radios, soon led to larger problems such as food and clothing shortages. Berlin's Jewish population no longer received ration coupons for meat or milk, and their clothing rations were restricted. Even worse, if one can imagine the situation being any worse, with the decrease in their rights, the Jews of Berlin and other parts of Europe faced an escalation in violent acts against them. Their struggles went beyond random acts of anti-Semitism. The harsh treatment they endured came at the hands of their own government and those who partnered with them, the very people most of them turned to for protection.

In Berlin, according to Horst, uniformed and armed Nazi soldiers roamed the streets in bunches of six to eight, and if they suspected someone was Jewish, they stopped and asked for his or her *Ausweis* (registration). When they saw the J on the card, they might bark, "What are you doing here you dirty Jew, dirtying up our clean streets?" Next, came the shoving around, pushing the person from one soldier to the next, and then, "They beat the living crap out of you." Many Jews were beaten to the point of collapse right there on the street and died from the brutal beatings. (Stern, 2006)

Horst learned that to be even remotely safe, they had to prove that their bloodline hadn't been tainted for the last eight generations. As a result, even quite a few Christians ended up in concentration camps, even though they had lived their entire lives as Christians. The Nazis determined the criteria for defining a person as a Jew. Everyone carried something similar to a passport, the Ausweis mentioned above, on which they were profiled. Each card reflected the name, address, religion, and so on. If the card belonged to a Jew, it was stamped with a big J on it. Horst discussed this when he wrote of it in 2006.

"The Nazis were masters at profiling. The way you looked? If you had a big nose they smelled a Jew behind it. The color of your eyes, your ears, whatever they made up in their minds, made you become a Jew.

If the suspected Jews did not have their registrations with them, they would be rounded up and held until such time that they would be taken away by truck on the first leg of their trip to a concentration camp. Many other citizens appeared not to care, and those non-Jewish Germans who might have felt compassion did not dare to intervene because aiding a Jew was second not only being a Jew but was also punishable by deportation to a concentration camp. Soon, Nazis began to drag Jews directly out of their apartments, usually in the middle of the night, and many were never seen again." (Stern, 2006)

At home, with Robert and Felicia, plans were formulated to leave Berlin. Robert, his wife, and Horst had papers in the works to immigrate to China. Everything was in order, except for one travel-through visa. Robert told Horst the name of the country that denied them that visa, but he has since forgotten it. The whole deal fell through, even though quite a few German-Jews succeeded in getting there and were able to survive the war. So, his uncle reverted to a back-up plan, which was to follow his parents to Budapest, Hungary. It was 1940 and, as Jews continued to disappear by the thousands in Berlin, they were still relatively safe in Hungary and as of then, had been left alone.

One day, Robert came home and told his wife that they were leaving immediately. When Felicia complained that she wasn't ready yet, it was the first time Horst saw his uncle lose his patience and yell at her, "I just got word from a friend that the Gestapo is on its way to pick the three of us up!" Obviously, she took his warning seriously because Horst had never before seen his aunt move so quickly. Fortunately, his aunt was prepared and had the absolute necessities already packed. They each picked up whatever they could and got out of there.

Robert was smart to leave his option open to go to Hungary because after they departed to Hungary via Prague, Czechoslovakia, Robert called Berlin and was informed that two days after they left, the Nazis were at the door of where they had lived to arrest them.

Years later, after the war in 1946, Horst returned to that house. After identifying himself, someone stepped forward and said, "I remember you. How did you know when to leave? You weren't gone for 20 minutes when the Gestapo showed up asking about your whereabouts. Stroke of luck." They stayed in Prague for a week with Felicia's cousin before continuing on by train to Budapest, Hungary.

When they arrived in Budapest, Horst's grandmother and his mother, Erna, picked them up from the train station. He was 12 years old at that time and had no recollection of what his mother looked like from the meeting in Berlin so many years prior, so he didn't recognize her. He also had no idea when his mother found her way back to her family and how it was that they decided to welcome her back after throwing her out when he was born. Yet there they stood, mother and daughter, together, the woman he cherished more than life itself and the stranger who gave birth to him. Where would he fit into their world?

Erna had secured a place for her brother Robert and his wife to live, and Horst was expected to reside with his mother and grandparents, and so it was that after living with them for the past two years, he parted with his uncle and aunt for good. He saw both of them now and then, just less frequently. They came over to visit, but the close relationship he had with his uncle was once again over.

They didn't have enough money to rent an apartment, so Horst, Erna, and his grandparents lived in a rented room at Kiraly Utca 23. Horst never knew if they paid rent or if they were a charity case, but the place in which they stayed wasn't exactly a room, but more of a huge kitchen.

Their little home had an oversized cast iron slab, on which they could heat enough water to bathe the whole family. This cast-iron slab had four round openings that came with four cast-iron rings of different sizes as one fitted into the other to accommodate the size of the pot. They could fry a couple of eggs on one opening and cook something else on the other simultaneously. The stove easily accommodated large pots of water for doing laundry and bathing water. Best of all was the heat it provided in winter. However, that same heat in the summer left their room feeling like a sauna.

In the kitchen there was also a table that could easily sit a dozen people, two single beds, one for his grandparents (until his grandfather died that same year) and one that he shared with Erna, two chairs, and one small commode cramped into a corner. It was a large room, but not a luxurious one. The room they shared changed by night. When darkness descended, it was overrun with cockroaches. At first, this repulsed Horst but within a few weeks the Sterns adapted because there was no other option for them. So prevalent were the bugs that when Horst had to go to the bathroom, he had to shake out his slippers first, but eventually he got to a point where he barely noticed them. One can get used to many less than ideal circumstances if one is poor, especially when there is no choice. Putting things into perspective, he realized it was still better than sleeping in the street. Certainly, they weren't living in a healthy environment for a young boy. More than just disgusting for the family to look at or walk on, the roaches carried filth and the risk of disease with them.

Izsak Stern finally succumbed to his illness, Tuberculosis, that year. Heavy with bitterness, Horst often reflected over the years that his grandfather was one of the few people in his family, from that point on, who would die of natural causes and not at the hands of the Nazis. Selma would later also die in her own bed, but not all of her siblings fared so well. Her two brothers were beaten to death in the streets of Berlin, and three of her four sisters were deported to and later murdered in Theresienstadt/Terezin concentration camp. One sister survived in Paris, France.

Once her father died, Erna was lucky enough to find another room in a four-story apartment house not far down the street, only ten houses down from where they had been living. In their new building, each floor housed five apartments that surrounded a courtyard. Three families had to share one bathroom. Bathhouses were located nearby, and water was often heated for sponge bathing. For the next five years, they hardly had enough money for food or rent, so trips to the bathhouse were a rare luxury.

For cooking, they used a kerosene air pressure cooker. There was only room for one pot at a time, so they ate many soups. The winters were cold, but they used a small potbellied stove in the room for warmth. When they wanted fresh bread, it was cheapest to make their own dough and then take it to the bakery where they charged a small fee to bake it in one of their large ovens. Selma trusted Horst to run that errand only once.

"The first time I was sent on that errand was also the last time. You see, when I picked up that still warm bread I committed the outrageous sin of eating almost half the loaf on my way home. Whatever possessed me to do that, was that first, I was hungry, and second, it just smelled and tasted too good, that once started I could not stop. If you have ever eaten bread right out of the oven, you will know what I am talking about." (Stern, 2006)

The apartment in which they rented their room belonged to a little old Jewish lady, who made her living renting out bed space. In order to get to their room, they first had to go through the kitchen and then the living room before they reached their room. The living room was occupied by the landlady, who slept in her bed. Three other people slept on cots that were put out each evening and put away during the day, and the same thing happened in the kitchen each night.

When there was a full house, there were 12 people there each night. The beds were rented on a weekly basis, but Horst's family paid monthly. Horst was the only male in the bunch and the only one who owned a gun, although he wasn't yet old enough to shoot it. All of the renters were women in their early thirties to early forties. Some of them worked at night in what he calls "the world's oldest profession." Even at a young age, he realized that they lived in do-or-die times, and that those who "did," had a higher chance of survival than those who didn't.

Even though approximately a dozen people resided there at night, plus at least another four who took the dayshift, they still somehow all managed to live there quite harmoniously.

There was no room for fighting or yelling, and they all realized that they were in the same boat, so why make waves. As crowded as that little apartment was, it was big in comparison to some living situations to come.

Unfortunately, in addition to the crowded conditions, and another cock roach infestation, they had bedbugs and there was no escaping them. Reflecting on such squalid living conditions could easily bring a person to the depth of depression and hopelessness, but Horst took the situations life handed him in stride. Of the bedbugs he lightly quips, "Every house and every apartment had them, and they didn't discriminate on the basis of social status; they plagued both rich and poor. The only difference was that the food was better in the rich neighborhood. They were equal opportunity bloodsuckers." The only way to get rid of them was by fumigation. Private dwellings generally got tented individually. This, however, wasn't a private dwelling, and the Stern family was painfully poor.

Imagine being so poor that you can't afford to keep clean. Although they had a sink and running water, it ran only cold water, making winters miserable. This was Horst's reality, but they did the best they could with what they had. All these years later, he holds an image in his mind of when his grandmother would wad up a piece of newspaper and walk the half-a-floor distance when she "had to go." It is a convenience that perhaps many people don't think about when they read about life for inmates in the concentration camp system, but those Jews who had already been taken to camps didn't even have the luxury of using newspaper for this purpose. The lack of toilet paper in the camps was just one of many methods used by the Nazis to dehumanize the Jews.

As challenging as times were, the situation for the Stern family continued to worsen in the months and years to come. Yet, when many Holocaust survivors could be bitter, Horst has always been grateful for having a strong constitution that allowed him to overcome the hardships. He encountered many who couldn't, especially the elderly.

Some 60 years after the war, Horst, by that time known by the Americanized version of his name, Henry, took his wife, Barbara, to Budapest on vacation to show her where he lived for six years during the Second World War. Nothing much had changed. The house where he lived still stood, and they were able to go inside.

Upon arriving, the Sterns even found one of the tenants from his time there who still resided in the building, a Mrs. Klistinets, whose husband was responsible for saving Selma's life twice when the Hungarian Nazis tried to take her away during their round-up of Jews at the house in 1943. Mrs. Klistinets was in her nineties at the time of their visit. Since so many years had passed, and it had been so long since he had spoken Hungarian, communication proved difficult, but he saw a little spark of remembrance in her eyes for a moment, but it went out as he continued talking. He realizes though that she tried very hard to remember who he was.

4

SCHOOL DAYS

While still living in the giant kitchen, Erna was working for a family taking care of a boy about the same age as Horst, cleaning the house and teaching him to speak German. She was able to take Horst along, which turned out great. He had someone to play with, and each boy benefited by learning each other's language. The people she worked for owned a shoe store, and Erna was able to enroll Horst into a private Jewish school thanks to their help, for gratis most likely, as his own family would never have been able to pay for it themselves. Reflecting on the opportunity now, he feels there was a Jewish organization that helped out those who needed it then, and that perhaps the Sterns had taken advantage of that as well. Since Horst didn't speak Hungarian, he was held back in school for two years. Therefore, he was 12 years old and still in the fourth grade, together with children who were ten years old. He was the tallest kid in the class and all of the other students around him were speaking in a language he didn't understand. While learning Hungarian, Horst obviously stuttered, but when he started to pick up a Hungarian word here or there, he noticed that his stuttering almost disappeared, except when he got excited, which admittedly, was quite often. He now says, "Then, I was the only kid who was able to stutter in two languages."

It wasn't long before he got into trouble for fighting and Erna was told that she would have to find another school for Horst. Somehow, she got him enrolled in another private school. Once again, the pattern repeated itself, and eventually, Horst was enrolled in a boys-only public school where he slowly began to learn the language, beginning with all of the cuss words. It took him two years to learn to speak fluent Hungarian but with a German accent. For the first year and a half, he didn't have any homework from school because he had a difficult time learning the language. The staff of this school were clearly not going to tolerate some of the behavior that exhibited Horst toward the other students. Here, punishment was swift and certain. Usually, it consisted of standing against the wall facing the teacher with both arms bent at the elbow and palms facing up. The teacher would take his/her ruler and whack the insolent student with it, hitting the open palm. Generally, one received ten whacks on each hand.

A second popular punishment was for the student to go to the first row and lean over a desk while looking at the other students, who sat there while the teacher took a switch, that he had for these special occasions, and whacked the perpetrator on the hind end. He would administer no fewer than three whacks.

It wasn't long before young Horst got the opportunity to experience this swift and sure discipline first-hand. He remembers that he went crying to his grandmother and told her what had happened. To his astonishment, his grandmother slapped his face and told him that this slap was for not listening to the teacher, and the teacher most likely had good reason to do what he did. That was the last time he complained at home about it, but certainly not the last time that Horst was disciplined at school. Classes were crowded, consisting of 50 to 60 students; yet, from the time when the teacher entered at the rear of the room and by the time he arrived at the front, every one of those students were silent. Some teachers were feared, but all were respected. Students generally didn't talk back, and most importantly, the school had the full support of the parents whenever discipline was necessary.

One teacher left a lasting impression on Horst, a teacher he nicknamed "The Sadist." This title was bestowed upon him because of the evil smile that would adorn his face after he had administered punishment. It was as if he thoroughly enjoyed it. To his credit, he managed to get the job done. The discipline was tough, but it helped form young Horst into the man he would one day become, and he knows that most of the time, he deserved what he got. In a recent conversation, he discussed the differences in today's school discipline, and lamented over a few of the changes. More than once, some of the kids came to school scratching their heads constantly, and within a week, most of the others followed suit. The teacher sent some of the kids to the school nurse who found out that most of them were infested with head lice. The clever teacher had a solution to the problem though; he declared that if any student came to school the next day without having his head shaved, he would be sent home. Parents who balked at this soon changed their minds with the untimely return of their children after having been turned away from school.

Ironically, this tough and "sadistic" teacher was the only one who realized that Horst had a speech defect and looked after him, making sure that he got into speech therapy class, which was held for kids just like him. This was the first time he met some other children with the same problems he had. Speech class was conducted three times a week after school. Horst couldn't really tell if it helped him or not. He thinks that perhaps his stuttering slowed down some, but he still stuttered. However, as he got older and began to learn another language, it eventually improved.

School can be a challenge for any student, especially when one must begin a new school in a new country, but Horst's hurdles were exacerbated by language issues, a severe speech impediment, and extreme poverty. He got little sympathy at home. The Stern family expected him to behave and to succeed regardless of their circumstances. This was easier said than done for Horst. His school days would continue to be trying times for him.

5

BECOMING A MAN

Shortly after arriving in Budapest, Horst approached his mother about the possibility of him getting an afternoon job to help contribute to the family financial situation. Knowing how scarce money was for the Sterns, Erna agreed. Soon, Horst became a delivery boy for a store that specialized in reconditioning hats by cleaning and blocking them, so when they were finished, they looked like new. The store sold men's hats as well. Those were the days when men generally wore hats, as demonstrated in most old movies. Horst was paid for each delivery he completed and he also received tips from the customers, without the need to speak much at all, other than to say hello in Hungarian, *Jonapot Kiwanock*.

At the same time, Horst was hired by the people who owned the vegetable store. Here, he had to clean up after closing each night. He was also allowed to take home all the fruit that was damaged, either from being mishandled by the customers or from getting squashed during transport. Regardless of the condition, the food was a welcomed blessing in the Stern household as his grandmother concocted meals using techniques such as dicing squashed fruit, putting it into water with sugar, boiling it, and letting it cool. They then had to eat it at room temperature because their "refrigerator" only worked in wintertime. It consisted of a shelf outside the window, which provided little room for temperature adjustment. It was either cold, or it was colder.

Whatever money Horst made went directly to his grandmother, the family financier, who could put up a meal with so little that it didn't surprise him that they could survive all those years. Selma closely guarded what little income they acquired and made it last for as long as possible.

Later, his Uncle Robert, who was quite a successful salesman for a company specializing in importing and selling small electric machinery, got him a job. One of Robert's customers needed a delivery boy who was able to pedal a large three-wheeler bicycle to deliver and pick up machinery around town. Erna worked endlessly too. The struggle to put food on the table and survive from day to day continued, but Horst didn't realize what a struggle it was at the time that they were living through it. Times were even harder than the young boy realized.

However, it didn't appear that all of the Sterns were struggling. The fact that Uncle Robert and his wife were doing very well for themselves didn't escape Horst's notice. Once, when he visited them at their apartment, he couldn't help but detect a bunch of Italian salamis, other sausages, and even a ham in their pantry. Meanwhile, in addition to their fruit soups, Horst, Erna, and Selma were living on chicken soup made out of chicken feet, heads, necks, and even the combs of the roosters and wing tips. Basically, they were sustained by all the items the green grocer couldn't sell, due to either being squashed or slightly spoiled. Once washed and trimmed, these items wound up in his grandmother's chicken soup and miraculously, no one ever got sick from it. To this day, he still does not know whether or not Robert ever helped them out financially once he no longer lived with the family.

Shortly before Horst turned 13 years old, the time in a boy's life when he is considered a man, his mother informed him that she decided he should have a Bar Mitzvah on his thirteenth birthday. Erna didn't ask, nor care about his opinion on this decision. He was simply informed that for the next three months, he would have to attend Hebrew school where he would learn the procedures and prepare himself for the ritual to come on that life-changing day.

While Horst resented having to go through all of this after a hard day at school, he was grateful that is was only for three days a week. He went to Hebrew school and was told by the rabbi that he would have to learn the prayers to recite in Hebrew. Since the Hebrew alphabet is completely different from the one with which he was acquainted, he had to start from the beginning. Once he was able to put the letters together, words formed, and when the rabbi taught Horst the pronunciation, he mimicked him. The rabbi would slap him on the back and say, "Good boy." By the end, he was able to read what he had to read, without understanding a word of it. He claims it felt like a Catholic saying prayers in Latin, which most of the congregation doesn't understand, but the promise to go to heaven is there if they continue with their prayers. He asked the rabbi to translate what he was reading in Hebrew. The rabbi replied, "Never mind. You are doing all right."

In addition to his Hebrew and religious training, Horst had to undergo a circumcision procedure. Because of his sudden appearance in the world, this was something that Erna had obviously given little thought to when he was born, and now it had to be done for his Bar Mitzvah. The procedure meant that he was in the hospital for a week, which also meant he missed a week of school. Exactly who paid for this procedure and hospital stay remains a mystery.

When the big day finally arrived, the rabbi mumbled his part, and Horst mumbled his own. To this day, he has no idea what it was that he said and he states honestly now that he couldn't have cared less. Officially, he became a man that day but everybody still kept telling him what to do.

In 1942, as his language skills continued to improve, Horst was eventually able to move ahead a level in school. His stuttering had even improved, so he stuttered less when speaking in Hungarian than when he did in German. Yet, after a long consultation about his education, one to which he wasn't invited, it was unanimously decided that he would be better off finishing his education in a trade school. Within three months, he received a certificate demonstrating his knowledge of a trade. However, he doesn't remember what that trade was, but he says that he must have been really good at it in order to receive a diploma in it.

Erna, working her magic once again, came up with another lead and it didn't take long before she had Horst working as an apprentice in a jewelry-making establishment. He worked amongst six men and one woman who made beautiful jewelry. Customers paid top dollar for unique pieces made of yellow, red, and white gold, all of which were worthy of display at Tiffany's in New York. This was the first time in Horst's life that he was really content, and he actually looked forward to going to work each day.

Initially, Horst's job consisted of running errands and sweeping the floor, but later he became more of an apprentice, as he too was taught to work with gold, brass, and copper to create jewelry. His inner artist awoke and working there led him to dream that one day he too would be able to create something of beauty like these people were able to do, but that dream was cut tragically short.

6

FORCED LABOR

Compared to Jews in other parts of Europe, with the exception of some difficulties imposed upon them, the Jews of Hungary had been left relatively unscathed. Suddenly, the situation changed, and the Hungarian Nazis began picking up young Jewish men against their will, taking them from their homes and from the streets. Particularly targeted were men more or less between the ages of 16 and 50. The captives were first marched to a collection station. Then most of them ended up somewhere in Russia after a long journey which many didn't survive.

Those who survived the trek, ended up in labor battalions within in the German army, where they were tasked with doing the most grueling jobs but were also used to prevent German troops from being blown up. One of their jobs was to look for and dig out mines in minefields. They also had to dig foxholes and supply ammunition to the frontline under fire. In other words, those conscripted were forced to perform the most dangerous tasks making their chances of survival fairly low. Their lives didn't matter and they were considered expendable. They were also known as cannon fodder. Not surprisingly, considering the treacherous tasks forced upon them, many of these Jews never made it back home.

Horst watched as the jewelry shop lost one employee after

another until finally only one remained. Lost seems such a mild word to describe the events of this time though. We must remember that in reality, each of these people was forcibly removed until only one man remained who hadn't been picked up. He was spared only because, for the moment, he was able to prove that he wasn't of the Jewish faith. With the only other remaining person in the shop, the owner, being Jewish, the store had to close, and he simply vanished.

After the war, Horst tried to find out what happened to his former jewelry store co-workers, but his search was unsuccessful, and he is quite sure they were all taken and killed. When he reflects on it all of these years later, he still can't understand how anyone could extinguish all of that talent. So many lives lost for no reason, other than for their religion.

Not long after Horst lost his job, Erna lost hers, causing even more hardship for the struggling Stern family. They tried in vain to find replacement jobs but people who used to hire day laborers stopped hiring. Many of them disappeared as they too were picked up off the streets or forced out of their apartments and on to waiting trucks. No one really knew if they would return.

Horst later learned that the people who were rounded up by the authorities could take two small suitcases with them to the location where they would perform light labor. They were assured that when the war ended, they would be safely returned to their homes and belongings. They had no choice but to believe what they were told and it was this belief, or perhaps their false hope, that aided the Hungarian police and the Nazis in gathering the Jews with some degree of cooperation and minimal resistance. Had their victims truly known what faced them, perhaps there would have been more of a fight. In reality, their belongings were taken from them, and very few of these Hungarian residents were ever seen or heard from again.

One might wonder why the victims believed what they were told so readily. In those days, according to Horst, the Jews of Budapest had no idea what was really going on in Europe. Slave labor battalions, ghettos, concentration camps, and crematoriums were all unbelievable rumors. After all, people in civilized countries didn't do that to each other. By the end of the war, Horst and his family knew of the reality of these atrocities all too well.

In order to help the family to survive, Erna began to walk to the district where the more affluent Jewish people lived, and after swallowing her pride, she knocked on doors. To those who answered, she either asked for work or for a handout. Usually, she was handed a few coins. It was amazing how fast word got around among the unfortunates. "Try that house, on such and such a street. It is good for 50 Filler or maybe a whole Pengo." So, Erna wasn't the only one who went door-to-door looking for help. Still, most thought that it couldn't possibly get worse, but it did. Soon those who answered the door and offered help also began to disappear. Some were fortunate enough to buy their way out, but most suffered the same fate as the others who had been forcibly removed. (Stern, 2006)

The Sterns were living in turbulent times, walking a fine line between life and death and never knowing which day might be their last, or if they would have anything to eat. Like many others, as desperation set in, they began to take food without paying for it. Mainly, they would take small items, a potato here, small vegetables there, never too often at the same store. Needless to say, Horst continued to do all that he could to help support his family. Every penny he was able to earn continued to go to the family banker, his grandmother.

When Erna came home from a day of knocking on doors, she handed all but some cigarette money to Selma. Smoking was a vice that Erna had been unable to give up, despite their dire financial situation. As the keeper of the funds, Selma would count the take for the day and decide what they could and should buy for that day. Unfortunately, there were many days that they went to bed hungry.

There was one exception to the strict austerity program under which Selma ran the household. One indulgence was permitted that served as a distraction from the hunger and misery that consumed them daily. It was the Saturday matinee. This weekly treat, just two hours, kept the three of them going. There, they saw mostly American movies with stars such as Judy Garland, Mickey Rooney, Greta Garbo, Spencer Tracy, and all the other stars in the movie industry. They particularly enjoyed the musicals. As they watched the films, they dreamed of a better life and they never wanted those movies to end.

Despite the fact that they were spending much needed food money for the privilege, the Sterns continued this indulgence until the showing of American movies was banned in 1943. Horst was surprised that they made this sacrifice but felt that Selma probably realized the importance of keeping their spirits up as well as their stomachs full.

Hungary allied itself with Germany in 1938, so compared to its neighboring countries in Europe, Budapest was a relatively safe place for Horst, his family, and other Jews to live. Until March of 1944, at which time the Germans made some changes. They installed a new Hungarian government led by Ferenc Szalasi, the leader of the anti-Semitic Arrow Cross Party.

The changes came quickly. First, there was a decree that all Jews were to wear the yellow Star of David on the left side of their outer garment so they could be easily identified. Anyone refusing to do so, would be arrested and imprisoned immediately, and consequently deported. Then came the closing of all Jewish stores and businesses, but Horst noticed that instead of destroying everything, the Germans just put their own men into them and continued to run the businesses.

Around the Stern family, the hunt for the Jewish population was on as the Hungarian Police, in conjunction with the German SS, began rounding up Jews all over the country. Upon their capture, they were loaded onto freight trains, which were then sealed from the outside.

Finally, they were taken to one of the many German camps set up throughout Europe, mainly Auschwitz in Poland. Later, rumors circulated that people were being killed in these camps, but by this time, their senses had been dulled to the point that only the immediate family mattered. The thought of giving up never entered their minds. They just existed day to day, one day at a time.

In late 1943, American pilots dropped bombs over Buda. A grain storage facility and many houses were destroyed. Horst, now 15 years old, watched the planes from the Pest side of the river and has never forgotten the "awesome" sight or experiencing the explosions.

The situation soon worsened for the Sterns. One morning, all tenants were called downstairs by the superintendent of the house in which they lived. He had been ordered by the Nazis to create a list of all the Jewish tenants of the house, their age, and their gender. Approximately 90 percent of the tenants were Jewish. This list had to be turned into the Nazis, who by then were fully in charge of the city. This scenario was repeated in apartment buildings all over Budapest. Armed with this information, the Nazis called up all males between the ages of 15 and 60 to be inducted into labor battalions. They had to be ready for the truck that would transport them the next morning to Buda, where American bombings had taken place earlier. The group of Jewish men would be put to work cleaning the mess.

Naturally, due to his age, Horst was among those forced to serve as free labor for the Nazis. For his first task, he was handed a sledgehammer and told to climb to the top of a concrete pile. There, he had to break up the big pieces into small enough pieces for one person to carry. Others started loading the truck from the bottom. They had one guard, a Hungarian soldier, apparently too old for the front line. The Jewish workers could see that he didn't care for the job he was told to do; his heart wasn't in it. Uncharacteristically of the soldiers in charge, he never demanded that anyone work harder. Horst even saw him take pity on an older man, in his sixties, and told him to find himself a place away from the street, where he couldn't be seen resting, and to come back to work whenever he felt up to it.

The workers had been told to bring their own lunch and those who could afford it were allowed to visit a store that was nearby on their lunch break. After ten hours of breaking up concrete, they were finally released for the day. They weren't provided a ride back home but were expected back by seven o'clock the next morning.

They were warned not to be late or there would be consequences. Horst chose the streetcar for his ride home, but unable to afford the fair, he rode on its bumper.

The next day brought another ten-hour day, but with fewer men. Some of the older men took a risk and stayed home. A new guard, who appeared to be no older than 18 years old, soon replaced the old guard. His full uniform made it evident that he was a member of the new Hungarian Nazi Party. Full of self-importance, this young guard felt the need to prove to his superiors that he was a more dedicated Nazi than his predecessor. He took pleasure in kicking those who didn't work fast enough. As the new guard would yell, "Work faster, faster, you dirty Jew," and relentlessly kick his victims, Horst watched helplessly knowing there was nothing that he could do to stop it.

One day as the Jewish workers assembled in the courtyard, the house superintendent relayed the message that there was no work for that day. He further told them that they should prepare themselves to leave the next day. They were told to have some food, a blanket, eating utensils, and a tin can out of which they could eat. What the message didn't say was for how long they should prepare to be gone for.

At six o'clock the next morning, two young Nazis arrived. They barked orders at the workers to get them to line up in twos and to start marching. Horst noted of the guards:

"One of them was a good looking, slim, blond man, at least 6'4 tall, the epitome of the perfect Aryan. His counterpart was the exact opposite. At 5'4" tall and dumpy looking, they made quite a sight standing next to each other. Both appeared to be in their twenties. But the most memorable and unforgettable thing about them was that they always carried a loaded pistol in their right hands, ready to use them at the drop of a pin." (Stern, 2006)

Before the men were marched off, the women had been told to return to their apartments and to not show their faces. Having said their goodbyes earlier, they followed the instructions as the men started to march out under the orders of the two Nazis. All was silent.

Meanwhile, Erna and Selma were left without the man of the family. As young as he was, Horst had taken care of the women in his family and had worked hard at odd jobs to contribute the much-needed money to the family coffers. Without him there, the Stern women's struggle intensified, and as fear of the unknown engulfed them, they worried endlessly about Horst.

7

THE MARCH

Approximately a dozen Jewish men set out on the march with Horst. He was the youngest of the group. The oldest was in his late sixties, but those numbers changed almost immediately. As they walked down Kiraly Street, other Jews joined them until they soon numbered into the hundreds. Horst realized what a sorry sight they were. Officially, the age was supposed to be from 15 to 60 years old but if someone was able to walk, it looked like he was taken to work regardless of age.

The two Nazis who picked Horst and the other men up left a lifelong impression on him. Both trigger-happy soldiers were quick to threaten the group with shots in the air or near their feet to keep them moving at an acceptable pace. Both types of shots accomplished the same result. The pace quickened. As the number of men in the march increased, they were split into groups of 30 or 40.

The people from Horst's house stayed together, and unfortunately, ended up in the same group as the original two Nazis. As soon as they were separated, the two guards started to herd them across one of five bridges that straddled the Danube River that separated the two parts of Budapest. They were leaving Pest and approaching Buda.

Darkness had fallen before the guards told them that they were done for the day. Under a sky full of stars most of them took their blankets and dropped to the ground in a field. They ate whatever food they had brought with them, and then most dropped immediately off to sleep after such a long and exhausting day.

A sudden and loud noise pierced the darkness. It turned out to be the guards, who by this time had been nicknamed Long and Shorty by the group, firing their pistols. They informed the group that if they ever heard more than two shots, it meant that one of the Jews had finally reached his final destination. It was their not-so-subtle way of saying that they better rise early. It was quite a wake-up call each day. From that day on, most of them were awake before they even heard the first shot. It played hell with Horst's system.

"I almost learned to sleep with one eye open. Five a.m. - no breakfast, just up." (Stern, 2006)

After three days and covering a distance of about 50 kilometers (approximately 31 miles), the weary group reached a big tent-like structure, devoid of cots, but it provided dry ground. At last, they had reached their destination. They did as they were told and settled in under its protection. After a while, they were instructed to start gathering stones and rocks and start building a small wall in a perimeter of about 25 feet around the structure that would be their home. Next, the guards told them to dig a latrine. Once that was completed, they were surprised as a truck pulled up with a couple of containers, which they were ordered to unload.

A pleasant surprise awaited them when the workers discovered the containers held hot soup, and the boxes that accompanied them were filled with bread. With that, the group of Jewish forced laborers received the first hot meal since leaving home. As they devoured the treasure, Shorty announced that anyone seen outside of the perimeter of the wall they had just built, at any time, would be shot on site. There was no reason to doubt what he said. Long was just looking for someone to do something wrong. He was quiet, but no one wanted to take the chance of finding out what he was capable of doing. Unfortunately, it wasn't too long before they found out anyway.

Shorty wasn't to be doubted either. He loved to hear himself yell, and he kept his pistol in his hand to help prove every point. They ate their meatless soup, which was supposedly cabbage and potato. At least it was hot and following it, they received a small piece of bread. They were told that this piece would have to last them until the next evening because all they would get in the morning was some hot coffee.

Two shots awoke Horst from his heavy slumber. Although it was still dark, he arose at once and put on his shoes to complete the outfit in which he had slept. Warm water to wash with was a distant memory. The last time he had seen any was the day he had left on this adventure, and although he couldn't know it at the time, he wouldn't see it again for another three months.

Cold rain fell throughout one dreary fall day and Horst made do the best he could without the benefit of a towel or soap, making do with an old shirt to dry off. After drinking whatever hot liquid it was that served for coffee and eating some of the bread given to them the night before, the tools of their new trade were handed out. These consisted of pick axes and shovels. Lined up, three abreast, the workers started marching and after about three miles they were told, at last, that they would be digging tank traps there. Long and Shorty explained what was expected of them. They were warned that those who had any complaints about the arrangement could speak up, and he would guarantee that a bullet in the head would convince the rest of them to shut up and start working. So, their group of about 40 started digging.

Worse than the constant manual labor was the hunger. Their stomachs screamed to be fed, but there was nothing ever offered for them to eat during their long ten-hour workdays. Their hunger didn't matter to the guards. Their only goal was to be the first group finished. In order to accomplish their mission, the younger men worked harder to try to make up for the older men, who couldn't keep up the fast and demanding pace expected from the guards. The progress was never enough for those two, and at the end of the day they decided that the group hadn't done their share, the laborers wouldn't receive any food.

Two weeks after following this routine, one morning at roll call, two men were missing. They had tried to escape, and the remaining workers weren't given any food until they were found, which was within 24 hours. The escapees were brutally beaten. Shorty liked to pistol whip the slave laborers, especially while the victim was tied to a chair. The remaining laborers were made to watch this to make sure they understood what to expect if anybody else had ideas of trying to escape.

The deterrent was obviously not enough though, because unbelievably, within three days, another worker also attempted escape, but was recaptured even faster. He received the same punishment, after which the guards warned them that if anyone else tried to escape, when caught (and they promised that they'd be caught), he would be executed along with three additional people chosen randomly. This threat was successful and the escapes stopped.

Life continued as a cycle of work, exhaustion, starvation, and more work. The group ate if they were lucky enough to get something. Eventually, the soup changed a bit from time to time, and at closer inspection, they detected some potato peels or carrots in it. The main ingredient continued to be cabbage. Horst looked into the pot one day and noticed a pair of eyes staring at him out of the soup, but he didn't say a word.

Fatigue dictated that the group ate whatever they were given and then collapsed for the night. Eventually, the elderly just couldn't continue. By this point, they could hardly get up in the morning and it wasn't for lack of trying. Even Shorty's threats didn't work, and they simply collapsed. Soon afterward, this group of workers, who were no longer productive, were taken away by truck and were never seen by the remaining workers again.

After two weeks of ditch digging, another worker missed roll call. He was found quickly, and the guards made good on their threat. They began by selecting a camp leader a young man in his early thirties, to manage food distribution, camp cleanliness, and making sure that all orders were followed. His father was selected to assist him in these duties.

One evening, after returning from work, they were told that due to the carelessness of their leader, one of the men was able to escape. The guard clearly blamed the new camp leader, claiming that if the man in charge been more vigilant the escape wouldn't have happened. He announced he would have to pay for it with his life, at which time the father begged for his son's life to be spared. He went so far as to beg them to take him instead of the other two who had been randomly chosen. The two guards agreed and led the father and the son to the back to the latrine area and executed both of them. The remaining laborers heard four shots. When the guards returned from their heinous task, they selected four men to go to the back to start digging the grave.

Within a few days of this episode, the laborers were again on the move. After breaking camp, they worked all day, slept a few hours, then started walking to a new location. This new routine continued for about ten days. Sometimes, they got fed the usual soup. Sometimes, they didn't eat for 48 hours. All of the working, walking, lack of sleep, and hunger took their toll. More of the older men just collapsed on the roadside, and as Horst later found out, they were executed on the spot and thrown onto a truck to be disposed of elsewhere.

By this time, it was November 1944, they were all wracked with hunger, desperate for warmth, and had lost track of time. Horst worried about his mother and grandmother back home and he wondered if he would survive all of this and return to them, but he didn't give up hope. He had been fortunate to be young and somewhat strong enough to survive so far. What was once a group of 40 now contained just 15 men. Interestingly, it seemed that the skinniest of them had the easiest time surviving. The biggest and strongest were the first to succumb to their difficult situation.

The dwindling group ended up at the Ujlaki Brickyard in Obuda where they were met by the noise of at least a thousand people, ranging in age from approximately ten to 60 plus, sprawled on the floor of the great hall. Much like his own group, some of them had already been worked to the point of exhaustion. Others had been picked up off the streets of Pest. This time women had been taken as well as men.

Rumors spread amongst the detainees. People speculated that the Nazis planned to march the Jews to the Austrian border to get them out of the way. It was a distance of approximately 200 kilometers (approximately 124 miles). Walking 20 kilometers, roughly 12 ½ miles, a day for ten days would solve their Jewish problem. Once at the Austrian border, the Nazis had cattle cars waiting. Horst learned much later that once they reached the border, the Jews either ended up in Dachau, near Munich, or at Mauthausen concentration camp in Austria. The ones who were still strong enough to work were taken to Vienna to work in the construction and fortification around the city.

During the two days Horst and the others spent at the brick factory, they got fed the familiar potato peel and cabbage soup with something unidentifiable floating in it, but it was early December and cold, and the soup was warm and filled the hole in his stomach, albeit, temporarily. They were all hungry, all of the time. By this time, he couldn't even remember a time when he last had a full stomach.

While lying on the floor with noise all around him, Horst tried to fall asleep. Suddenly, he heard someone calling him, "Horst? Is there anybody here by the name of Horst Stern? I am looking for my son, Horst Stern." Other people started spreading the word, and before he knew it, the whole room was looking for him. At last, word reached him, and he was reunited with his mother, Erna.

Horst couldn't believe it. With the massive number of people who had gone through this brickyard transit camp in the past, the odds of one family member finding another one were slim.

Despite the nearly impossible chance of doing so, his mother found him within that sea of people. When Horst asked his mother how she wound up there, she told him that she had been at the bakery picking up some bread when a Nazi patrol came into the store and started picking up all the people who wore the yellow star, including Erna. They were put onto a truck and taken to the brick factory to be sent, just like all the rest, to the camps.

Horst could hardly wait to find out how his grandmother was doing. Erna put his mind at ease when she told him that considering the times, she was holding up all right but of course worried about him. Then Erna said that she had to get back to Pest because Selma had no idea what happened to her, but she knew that the other residents of the house were taking good care of her. He asked Erna how she would get back. She said that she would tell him about it next time. Then, Erna dug into her bag and produced a big piece of bread for him, the best present that he had ever received.

They said goodbye to one another and Erna went back to the group of people she had come with. Sometime later, he learned that when Erna didn't return from the bakery, the people in the house took care of his grandmother by making sure that she had enough to eat and trying to comfort her by telling her that Erna would be back shortly. The problem with that though was that they only spoke Hungarian, and Selma only knew two words of Hungarian. Erna knew that she had to return. When Erna and Horst parted that day, neither of them knew if it would be the last time they would be together.

Two days into his stay at the brick factory, it was time for at least 100 people to leave. They were told to line up for "a nice walk in the countryside." This was the beginning of what would later be known as the Budapest Death March. They walked four abreast from morning to night with few stops in between. They knew only that they were on the road leading to the Austrian border but not the fate that awaited them once they reached the border. Perhaps it was a good thing that they didn't know or they may not have gone so willingly.

There were other factors that led to the Jew's willingness to obey. First, many didn't realize, until the last moment, what was actually in store for them because they believed the lies that were told to them and by the time they realized they had been lied to, it was too late to do anything about it. Second, all they could think of was food. All of their senses were dulled and they weren't thinking clearly. All they could focus on was their next meal.

In this case, the Nazis continued to promise the Jews that they were getting close and would soon be able to eat and rest. They were also told that once the Germans had won the war they would be required to work but they would be reimbursed for their work and allowed to go back to the places they called home. The Jews, in their weakened states, believed these lies and marched on.

Six elderly Hungarian soldiers in uniform guarded those on the march, and the Jews noticed the guards didn't seem to agree with what was going on. By this point, there wasn't much discipline and the group was no longer in any strict formation. They were given occasional rest stops, here and there. Those who brought some food with them ate. Those who didn't have a chance to prepare for the journey either asked others to share or fell out of line to look over the farm fields they passed on the walk. Food was difficult to find as it was November. An occasional potato or cornhusk was usually all that could be found. There were some apple trees by the roadside, but the fruit was green, sour in taste, and in most cases, made them ill.

After that first day on the road, most of them waited for darkness to set in, so no one could see if they ate something or not, because if others knew, they expected the eater to share. Horst described it as,

"Entering the world of the beast- survival of the fittest. Because no one knew where the next meal would come from, you made sure that you looked after yourself first." (Stern, 2006)

As some people resorted to stealing, fights broke out, but that was only the beginning and it was only the second day on the road. There was no doubt that this behavior would only get worse as starvation intensified.

If any of them wanted to get out of line to relieve themselves, they had to raise their hand, catch the guard's eye, and they were allowed to go into the bushes, and then get back into line. They weren't required to catch up with the same people that they walked with prior to their break. After a long day of walking, the time finally came for them to stop and rest for the night and to their total surprise, they discovered that they would be stopping at a meadow where there was a camp awaiting them. Even better, there was a mobile field kitchen there to serve them soup and bread. They had long since learned to eat some immediately but save some for the next day.

Cold nights meant doubling and tripling up in an attempt to use body heat for warmth. This method worked for a while but if it started raining, sleep was impossible. The group was drenched right down to the skin and shivering. There was nowhere to go to get out of the rain, so they sat as close together as possible with blankets on top of their heads. Even in those circumstances, Horst was somehow able to catnap. It is amazing what the human body can withstand. Morning finally arrived, and after drinking the hot liquid that was supposed to be coffee they almost felt human again as the prepared for another long day of walking.

As Horst looked around him on day three, he started to realize that people he had seen during the previous days were missing. That's when he learned that once again some of the elderly had complained to the guards that they couldn't make it any further and were sent to sit at the edge of the road until a truck came by to pick them up at which time they were driven to some remote spot and executed.

That same day, Horst came across a young boy he recognized and who had lived in the same house as him and his family. When Horst asked him where his parents were, he explained that some Nylos (Young Nazi party members) picked him up as the result of seeing the star on his clothes as he was running some errands for his mother. He was forced onto a truck, as were others found walking on the streets along the way. Once filled, the truck transported them to the brick factory in Obuda.

Coincidentally, the young boy had the same last name as Horst but they weren't related. Still, Horst felt sorry and responsible for the tired and hungry boy. He was only about ten years old. Horst shared a bit of his own bread with him and tied a string around each of their wrists so the younger boy wouldn't fall behind or get lost in the crowd. Despite his best efforts to protect the younger boy, Horst lost track of him two days later. He still thinks of him and hopes he made it through.

After five days of walking, Horst decided to sneak away. He waited until everyone was asleep, excused himself from the people he was with, and backtracked for about 30 minutes. He found a big bush and crawled into it with his blanket to sleep. For the first time in over a month, he actually slept undisturbed until noon, despite how cold that night had been. He ate a small piece of bread that he had saved from the previous day and cautiously emerged from his hiding place.

As Horst started walking back the way he had come the previous day, he saw no one at all on the road. He felt relatively safe on a small dirt road he discovered and walked for quite a while before finding a large tree under which he finished the bread and napped. Sometime later, he was quite suddenly and rudely awakened by a couple of elderly soldiers kicking him lightly in the ribs.

They asked Horst why he was sleeping outside on the ground on a cold November day. He lied and said that he had run away from home in Budapest. After ordering him to grab his blanket, the soldiers escorted him to the nearest small town and took him to the police station. They told the man in charge, "Here is another one. He stinks even more than the one before."

Horst realized that he stunk and began to explain how one could hardly help but stink when he hadn't had a bath in a month, or more, and had no real toilet paper. He soon noticed that no one was listening to him. In the cell, there were three other boys who had told an almost identical story to Horst's. Fortunately, the soldiers that apprehended them were from a regular Hungarian Army unit. They too hated the Nazis, so they treated the boys with compassion and understanding. Their lives would have been in danger had the Nazis caught them, but the threat of that didn't deter them from helping the boys.

While in the jail, they were treated to the best meal they had in a long time, a Hungarian goulash soup with all the bread they wanted. Surprisingly, none of them got sick after eating such a rich meal even after having gone so long without real food. Another good meal was provided for breakfast the next morning. As odd as it might sound, Horst remembers this night in jail fondly for the kind treatment and good meals he received there.

The food and warmth didn't last though, the next morning one of the guards brought the boys to the main highway and soon after another group of prisoners wearing yellow stars shuffled by and the guard told the four boys to mingle with the rest of them. He also said that his little village is going broke from feeding the escapees they catch every day, so he didn't want to see them again.

The guards of the new group seemed oblivious to the fact that they had new members in their ranks. Horst had actually gained another day by backtracking, which turned out well for him. It didn't take long before he was hungry again, but his spirits were lifted when he came up with a plan that would change the course of his life.

Over the next three days, the guards started to drive them a little harder in an attempt to quicken their pace. Horst knew that they all looked like scarecrows and smelled even worse than they looked. He was convinced that, depending on which way the wind was blowing, anyone in front of them must have smelled them coming at least a kilometer before they arrived. Horst considered the situation he was in and decided it was time to activate his plan to attempt another escape.

His plan was pretty simple and might even cost him his life, but by this point, he felt he had very little left to lose. He would have to wait until they stopped to eat and sleep for the night, so he stretched out and waited until all was quiet. Everyone was so exhausted that they spent very little time in conversation and by the time it got dark, they fell fast asleep.

Quiet soon settled over the camp and stealthily, taking his blanket, Horst crept out of camp. Fortunately, camp had been established not far from where the Danube River flowed. His plan was to try to find a small dinghy to "liberate" and row over to the other side of the Danube River to get to Pest. He thought that he would avoid any army or police patrols as all the commotion was on the side he had just come from, Buda. He walked about three hundred yards and climbed down the embankment.

Approximately 45 minutes into his walk along the Danube River, he finally spotted a boat he thought might be small enough for him to handle. After untying the rope from the post, he jumped in, found a pair of oars, and tried to row the boat away from the shore and toward the center of the river. He soon realized though that this was a far bigger task than he bargained for. The boat was just too big for him to handle and he overestimated his strength. He had lost a lot of weight and wasn't in the same shape he had once been. As a result, the boat drifted back in the direction from which he had been walking with the others.

Despite his best efforts to steer the boat to the opposite side, it just wasn't possible, so he just sat there and let himself be carried by the current. He ended up almost back where he started, but he had drifted back by quite a few kilometers. Dawn was breaking when the boat finally hit the shore. He got out, climbed the incline, and ended up face to face with an army patrol.

Fortunately, no one connected Horst with the disappearance of a boat, and the patrol that picked him up didn't even ask what he was doing on the road. According to Horst, "All they had to do was smell me, and they knew where I was coming from. I was dirty, scrawny, skinny as a rail, with long hair. One of them even thought that I was a girl." Once again, he was taken to the town's jail. He was happy to arrive there just in time for breakfast. He ate and then flopped onto the cot and fell into a deep sleep. (Stern, 2006)

It seemed that only ten minutes had passed, when Horst was awakened by the guard. He was informed that vacation time was over, and he had a transport to catch. He gave Horst some sound advice:

"Listen to me kid. After today, we from the regular army are being sent to the front and those young Nylos are taking over. Some of them are not even 16 years old. They are wild, hate the Jews, and won't hesitate to pull the trigger. They won't ask you where you come from when you're caught. All they will do is beat you, half to death, and make sure they shoot the other half that is still alive. So, watch yourself." (Stern, 2006)

And after imparting this advice, he put Horst into the next bunch of people walking by.

As Horst looked around, he noticed an increase in the number of guards. Trudging ahead by forcing one foot after the other, hour after hour, he soon lost all sense of time, falling into a kind of trance. He didn't notice anything around him. He would snap out of it only when the column stopped and he stepped into the person in front of him. Exhaustion from each day was so complete that Horst was able to sleep through a night of rain. He would wake up in the morning wet and shivering but after drinking the so-called coffee, he would start to talk to himself for motivation to keep going. He would tell himself things like, "Horst, those bastards are not going to get you; you are going to come out of this mess alive." Then he would march on until they made their evening stop.

Eventually, they ended up by a big barge moored in place and learned that it was where they were going to stay for a couple of days of much-needed rest. Rumors began that they were just two days away from Austria. According to rumor, there would be a hot soup kitchen waiting for them and a heated train would take them to their final destination, no more walking.

While on that barge, Horst started to realize the toll the walk from Budapest had taken.

More than half of the group came down with dysentery. Here, he describes the results in his own straight-forward manner.

"Since there were no toilets, anybody who had to relieve him/herself just went to the end of the barge, dropped their pants, and let go. Since there was no bar to hold on to, he or she would ask the nearest person to please hold their hand, or to grab some of their clothing since the danger of falling into the water was there at any time. A lot of them had a hard time just to make it to the place..." (Stern, 2006)

In just the two days Horst was there, dysentery claimed quite a few lives. Typhoid rumors also circulated, but Horst didn't know if it was true. All he knew was that there was a steadily increasing number of dead people and more of them kept dying. They were all weak from the lack of food, exhausted, and lethargic to the point that without any fuss, some of them died on the floor right where they lay.

When they first arrived at the barge, *Das Totenschiff* (The Ship of Death), there had been remaining marchers from previous transports who were too sick to go on. Those who could still move went on to the next rest stop. Their nightmare would continue.

While there, Horst ran into people he had known from Budapest. Mrs. Dejoefi and her son had been friends with his mother and uncle. She was afraid that she wouldn't make it to the end of this ordeal, so asked if Horst would send her regards to his family when he next saw them. Perhaps she truly had known her fate because Horst never saw them again.

The rumor mill began again, and the word was that the next location would be their second last stop. Two days later, the group found itself at a collection station from where, in groups of 500 people, they would be sent to the border.

When Horst arrived there, one transport had just left the day before, and more people were expected shortly, but everything changed late that afternoon. A civilian car and two big trucks, displaying the Red Cross emblem on their sides and flying the Swiss flag, drove onto the campgrounds and came to a halt. A man in civilian clothing with a miniature Swiss flag in his lapel got out and demanded to talk to the commander in charge of the camp. The commander, angry at the man's intrusion, stepped forward and ordered that the man identify himself immediately.

Waving a folder of official-looking papers in the face of the commander, he replied that he was a citizen of Switzerland from the Swiss Embassy and a representative of the Red Cross. I suspect this may have been Swedish diplomat Raoul Wallenberg or a representative sent as a result of the rescue operations of which he played a vital part, but young Horst had no way of knowing this. He only knew that the man explained that he had papers from the highest authority. He turned and yelled at the men in the trucks to set up a table and chairs, reminding them that they were in a hurry and had a lot of work to do in a very short time. Facing the commander once again, the man told him that he was ordered to seek out all children, up to the age of 15 years, and to take them back to Budapest because other arrangements had been made for them.

As this was going on, five men in Swiss Army uniforms emerged from the trucks. As instructed, tables and chairs were immediately set up, and an announcement was made that all children up to the age of 15 needed to form a line and present any kind of identification they might have on them to prove their age. Those who had no papers would be asked a few questions and judged by the person at the table. After answering questions like the year they were born in, if they qualified, they could hop onto the truck. They were to leave all belongings behind.

Horst estimated there to be at least 50 to 60 kids in line and wondered how they all had identification papers, He certainly hadn't thought of taking any kind of identification when he was originally taken. Before he realized what was happening, someone put a piece of paper into his hand. Like a whirlwind, with new identification in hand, he was suddenly on the truck. The rear flap of the truck went up, and they were on their way. The last thing he remembered seeing before leaving was the look on the faces of those people left behind. They looked as if they knew that this was the last time they would see any of the youngsters again.

In record time, the truck crossed the distance that had taken the group so many days of walking, through misery, cold, and rain. As the truck was enclosed, they never really knew where they were at any given time until it stopped, the tarp was lifted, and they realized that they were back in Budapest in the Jewish quarter and had stopped in front of the Dohany Synagogue.

He can't recall how long the trip took. He said it could have been two, four, or even six hours because they were in the dark for the entire time. They were sent into the synagogue where they were fed and urged to sleep. After breakfast the next morning, they learned that they were inside the Budapest Ghetto.

Neolog Dohány Street Synagogue in Budapest, Hungary. Photo: Wikimedia Commons

8

THE BUDAPEST GHETTO

Enclosed by large walls, the Budapest Ghetto had six gates leading to the outside and was guarded by members of the Young Nylos. They monitored those who came in and those who left and made sure that nobody smuggled food in, but those who tried weren't the only ones subjected to beatings. There actually didn't need to be a reason for one to be pummeled. Furthermore, it was common knowledge that there was a standing order that if the war should take a turn for the worse and the Russians closed in, the Young Nylos were to blow up the ghetto with everybody in it.

News of the group's arrival spread like wildfire. As a result, parents soon appeared desperately looking for their children who had so suddenly disappeared from their homes. Those who found their children were overcome with emotion, ranging from relief to joy. However, the parents whose children didn't make it back were devastated. Refusing to give up hope, those parents asked every one of the new arrivals if they had seen their children.

Seeing those parents go home empty-handed was distressing. Equally disturbing was that there were some kids who came back to Budapest only to find that their parents were taken on one of the transports from which this group had just escaped. It didn't take long before Horst's own mother showed up, and relieved to find her son, quickly swept him away to the place where she was living. On the way there, Erna explained that after the day they had last seen each other and parted at the Obuda factory, she and others were put onto another transport and sent to Austria.

Erma shared the following explanation of her own experiences with Horst:

"There must have been 500 of us. We started rather early in the morning, and before the guards could organize us into columns of four, I took a chance and stepped out of line. As we were going past the houses, I looked and found a door that led into the basement. Nobody noticed me, since all was quiet, and by the time I had reached the cellar, all I could hear was utter silence. I did not see or hear anything except an occasional door slam. I must have fallen asleep; for when I opened my eyes, it was almost dark outside. I ate some of the bread I had on me, waited until it was completely dark, and just walked home. How I managed to do that, I have no idea. Lady Luck sure smiled on me that night.

When I reached the house where I lived, I found it locked for the night. But lately there was always one person at the front door for such an emergency. The house warden recognized me through the peephole, and the door was opened immediately. That's when I almost collapsed.

The people in the house had suspected what had happened and were happy to see that I made it back. They took care of Oma while I was gone, made sure that she had food, and tried to convince her that everything would turn out all right. Oma did not understand a word of what was said, but somehow she put on a brave face and made believe she understood.

In a way it was kind of funny, because when I finally got up those stairs, Oma said, 'You left two days ago to get some bread from the bakery. Now that you finally decided to come home, I see that you ate it all by yourself. Remind me not to send you out for anything anymore.' You should have seen her face when she saw me." (Stern, 2006)

Horst's grandmother had a sense of humor. By the time Erna finished telling her story, they had arrived at the apartment house where she and Selma had been housed with another ten people in one room. Horst asked her how they ended up there and Erna explained that not long after she was able to escape and arrived back home, the Nazis showed up again one morning and demanded that all Jews still living in the house go down into the courtyard and take only the things they could carry because they were being sent to a different place to live.

Erna gathered what little food she had left and as it was wintertime, she and Selma layered on as much clothing as they could wear. She then grabbed some family pictures and as much bedding as she could carry. By this time, there were only about six Jewish people left in the house, everyone else had been picked up at an earlier time.

Although Erna was the youngest in the building, she fit in easily with the rest of the older residents because of the way she dressed and her lack of makeup; she had to give up wearing it long before. Even though she was only 38 years old, she had the appearance of an old woman. Horst recalled,

"Erna wore a babushka, also called a scarf, around her head. No man in his right mind would have looked at her twice, make that once." In reality, stress had added years to each of them making them appear much older. They were all malnourished and filthy. It was difficult to get clean when all they had was cold water and it meant that they always smelled bad." (Stern, 2006)

Soldiers rounding up Jews in Budapest for deportation 20-22 October 1944. Photo: German Federal Archive

Fortunately, it didn't take very long to get to the place in the Ghetto. Carrying all the belongings they could, the group walked for about six blocks to their destination on Wesselany Utca. Each new resident was given an apartment number from the house warden in charge and they were directed to "their place," where they would reside until the end of the war.

As mentioned before, Erna and Selma were assigned to a room with ten other people. Selma was given a pullout couch, someone was kind enough to give it to her because of her advanced age. Instead, that person slept on a mattress under a table. There were other mattresses on the floor and two additional sofas. Someone even slept on the large dining table. Horst often wondered about the original owners of the apartment. Had they been forced out of it or had they escaped in time? There was no way, at that time, to find out their fate.

At least 30 people lived in the apartment, filling a bedroom, a kitchen, and a bathroom. Each floor of the six-story building held at least six or seven apartments, all of which contained a similar number of occupants. Once Horst arrived, he had to join his mother and grandmother on the couch.

Lying side by side by side didn't work out well for the three Sterns, so Horst stretched across the foot of the pullout couch, which meant that Erna had to pull her feet in a little bit to prevent her from kicking him off the end. With Selma, at under five feet tall, it wasn't an issue.

On Horst's second day in the ghetto sickness swept over him and sharing one bathroom with 30 people nearly caused a few accidents during his illness. Yet, as crazy as it might sound, the bathroom situation was an upgrade for the Sterns. They no longer had to brave the elements to use an outdoor bathroom, a great advantage in the winter months. Having a bathroom in the same apartment they lived in was a treat that they hadn't experienced since 1940 which was five years earlier in Berlin, it was now almost the end of 1944.

However, an indoor bathroom didn't ensure hot water. At the

bottom of the water tank, in the bathroom, was a place to light a fire and feed it with briquettes, pieces of wood, or at times, both. The fire heated the water in the boiler and before long there was hot water for a bath. Unfortunately, they didn't have the coal or the wood to make a fire. The stench of so many unbathed bodies in one place was indescribable.

Heat was an unavailable luxury in their apartment too, so most of them stayed in bed, under the covers. Yet, Selma never complained. By this time she was 78 years old. Considering her age, she did better than many of those who were younger than she was. She had always been the one who everyone in the family turned to with a problem. If her sisters needed something to be settled within the family, they ran to Selma. She was the strongest person Horst ever knew. She gracefully handled whatever life threw at her.

With very little to eat, life became strictly a question of survival. Self-preservation dictated that they take care of only the immediate family. The people in their apartment who shared in the beginning learned the hard way and came to the conclusion that you cannot always be generous because people take advantage of others. The food that people brought in was either consumed as fast as possible, before it was stolen from them, or they hid it where they slept until it was time to eat it. Once caring and kind, people quickly became self-centered and stopped sharing because there was no way of knowing what shortages they would face in the days to come.

Horst soon learned that a ghetto council had been established. With the help of the Swiss Red Cross, some soup kitchens were set up to try and make sure that the inhabitants would, at least, receive one hot meal each day which consisted of a bowl of soup and a ration of bread. The fact that they could bring in all that food for so many thousands of people made them heroes in the eyes of young Horst. A house warden was responsible for each ghetto house and it was that person's job to provide an exact count of the people who resided there. That count determined how much food their house received. The distribution station for their house was about three blocks down the street.

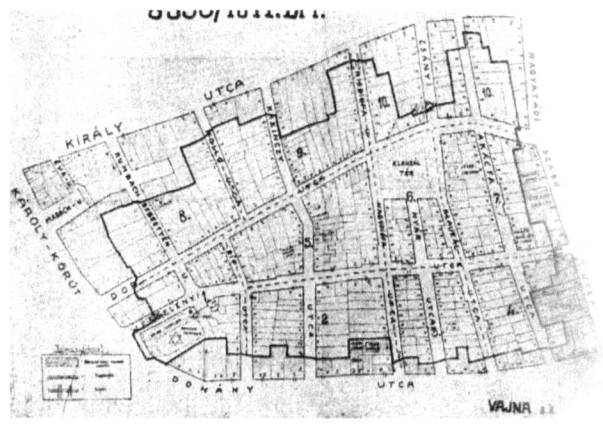
Contour map of the Ghetto of Budapest (1944) - Public Domain

When Horst learned that young and able volunteers were needed to help with picking up the rations for their house, he immediately volunteered, and by doing so, he was allotted an extra bowl of soup. The milk cans used for carrying the soup were heavy enough when empty but once filled they were difficult to carry and it took two men to handle the job. Yet, coming up with strength he didn't know he had because of his hunger, he carried out the task.

If there was one constant in the world of the Sterns, it was insecurity, and within a week of Horst's arrival to the Budapest Ghetto it took on a new form. Now, in addition to wondering where their next meal would come from, they wondered if they would even survive. The threat of death loomed and the first person to perish in their house was a little old lady. She looked healthier than the rest of them but for some reason was the first one to die. After her death was reported to the house warden, two men showed up with a casket, placed the woman inside, and carried her off.

The newly vacated space within the apartment was filled almost immediately with someone new. Although the apartment was bursting with the 30 people that occupied it, there were only two men, and Horst was one of them. Generally speaking, everyone was too busy looking out for themselves to form any friendships. However, Horst become friendly with the only other man who lived there with his wife. They appeared to be in their early fifties. It was truly miraculous for a man his age to have avoided being picked up and sent away like so many others and he attributed his luck to his clubfoot, confiding to Horst that this was the first time he was grateful for his disability.

The middle-aged couple resided on a mattress placed on the floor right in front of a credenza, the doors of which were always locked. They wondered what they might find inside if they had access to the key and envisioned it full of food. The very thought inspired them to try to get the cabinet opened. Horst suggested that they try.

In Horst's mind, there wasn't a moral dilemma because the people who owned the apartment and its furnishings weren't present. Any potential guilt could be reconciled by committing to, one day, reimbursing the owners, if that was ever possible. Under different circumstances, and had Horst and his partner-in-crime not been near starving, they may have seen that a moral dilemma did in fact exist. Despite their intentions, repaying the former residents wouldn't be necessary, and deep down they knew it. The previous family had most likely been forced to flee, or worse, had been taken involuntarily. Did that make stealing from them acceptable? Should the family's disappearance absolve Horst and his partner from guilt? Despite any apprehension, hunger again prevailed, and they decided it was necessary to try.

After waiting for what seemed like an eternity, everyone in the room finally succumbed to sleep and the duo vowed to repay the original occupants for any food they might find, if by chance they happened to survive the current circumstances. Continuing with their plan, they jimmied one of the doors open using a knife.

The anticipation was almost too much to bear for the starving men as they dug through pillowcases and blankets, but after reaching deeper they discovered at least two pounds of flour and a bag of sugar. Horst must have made some noise as he continued to search because one of the women in the room complained about the commotion. Horst, thinking quickly, spoke up and told her that he had stubbed his toe on the table's leg on the way to the bathroom. After she accepted his explanation, everything was quiet once again. They tried to close the door the best they could, and after they hid their treasure under the couple's mattress, he went back to the couch and went to sleep.

Horst and his partner almost got away with their plan, except an "eagle-eyed" woman detected a small trace of flour on the floor. She remembered the noise during the night and wanted to know what was going on and why it was there. As they were confronted, his partner's wife spoke up and told "eagle-eye" that she had dropped her face powder onto the floor and tried to wipe it up, and in doing so, she had smeared it a little. She said because it happened during the night, she had to wait for daylight to get some water to clean the floor properly. Fortunately, her quick thinking worked, and her explanation put an end to the confrontation.

For the time being, the flour and sugar were hidden under the couple's mattress, because it wasn't one of the mattresses that had to be moved during the day. This would only be a temporary solution though. Soon the men found a little hiding place in the cellar of the house and they began experimenting with making food from their new ingredients. Creatively, they worked to discover what could be done with only water, flour, and fire. Necessity being the mother of invention, they found some old bricks in the cellar and positioned them in such a way that they produced a small furnace-like cooking platform. With the means for cooking established, attention turned to finding anything that would burn and finally they started a little fire.

To create the least amount of smoke, the fire was kept as small as possible. Fortunately, they had a pot for heating water and a frying pan. The first culinary experiment they tried was putting some lumps of raw dough into the hot water. The result was cooked flour balls on which they sprinkled some sugar. They actually liked them and took some to Erna, Selma, and his partner's wife. Naturally, Erna wanted to know where Horst had gotten the ingredients from. Once he confessed, she suggested that it might be easier to make pancakes next time. They took her advice and although they wished that they had some butter or lard they were happy to have what we they did.

The food they created from their secret stash of flour and sugar saved their lives. Eating them at night helped them avoid detection so that no one else caught on to what they were doing. Under normal circumstances, it would have been natural for them to share with the other residents of the house, rather than avoid them, but with each passing day and each dying person, the need for self-preservation increased. Hard times had changed them, and now they were each forced to focus on their own needs. It was every man for himself.

Death descended upon the Stern family like a thick inescapable fog. People in the room, in the house, and in the ghetto kept dying, mainly from dysentery, poor nutrition, and dehydration. At first, for someone so young, the passing of one person after another both upset and frightened Horst. Soon, worry turned into apathy as the realization dawned that it was only a question of time before they too would succumb to death's grasp. It seemed there was no way to avoid it in such squalid conditions and with so little food. Clearly, it was just a matter of when, and not if, death would find each of them.

With so many dying, disposal of the dead posed a significant problem. Corpses piled up until, eventually, a call went out for volunteers to help and Horst answered the call. It's amazing how a person can adapt to new circumstances. For his efforts, he was paid in the most valuable currency in the ghetto, food. With the addition of the extra bowl of soup and piece of bread, for the first time in many years, the three Sterns felt rich because they now had steady meals. They ended up with five bowls of soup and plenty of bread because Horst still had his other job, picking up food from the distribution center.

As the Jewish holiday of Chanukah arrived, the house residents went through the motions of sharing holiday greetings but they mainly wished each other a happier one for the next year. In the room next to theirs, the bedroom, which was just as crowded as their own room, there were two elderly ladies, both in their seventies, who were prim and properly dressed. Neither of them were pleased with the holiday commotion, and rather than participate, one spoke up and said, "The Nazis made a big mistake when they picked us up and put us here in the Ghetto with all these Jewish people." Having converted some fifty years ago to Catholicism, the ladies had lived proper Christian lives and just couldn't understand why they should be considered Jewish. Hitler's decree held no regard for conversions and insisted that anyone with Jewish ancestry spanning less than eight generations had tainted blood and therefore was considered to be a Jew. One of the ladies graciously wished them happy holidays anyway. Sadly, both of them passed away shortly thereafter. (Stern, 2006)

One time, Horst sat watching an elderly woman for a while. She lay on her sofa, not far from him, and nibbled on a piece of bread. A day or two had passed since she had last gotten up and she held one arm up above her head and stared blankly up at the ceiling, her other arm rested at her side and when Horst looked closer he realized that she had died during the night. He gently lifted her onto her side and searched under her blanket until he found what he searched for, hidden food. There it was, almost a half a loaf of bread, which he gently took. It was a little moldy but still edible and he couldn't afford to be choosy. Acts such as these were unthinkable under normal circumstances, but in the ghetto, it was a common occurrence to which a second thought wasn't given. He reported her death and was told to find someone to help him dispose of her body.

By this time, the inhabitants of the ghetto disposed of the dead by unceremoniously throwing the corpses over a six-foot wall. They were told that there was an empty lot on the other side and although Horst never checked it out for himself, he recalls that no one ever complained, so he assumed that it was true. As the number of corpses began to mount, they were thankful that it was a cold, snowy winter. The corpses froze and it took them longer to decompose, keeping the stench to a minimum until gasses started to leak from them. To this day, he has never forgotten that smell.

During 1944, at 16 years old, Horst's life had become a never-ending cycle of fighting for food, working jobs no one else wanted, watching the people around him give in to death, disposing of their remains, and sleep. Hardship seemed to be all he had ever known, but he never gave in. Tirelessly, he labored to support himself, his mother, and his grandmother.

Walls of the ghetto, last section demolished in 2006 (Later reconstructed) Released under GFDL in the English Wikipedia by the photographer. https://en.wikipedia.org/wiki/File:BudapestGhettowall.jpg

The last remaining section of the ghetto wall in Budapest, rebuilt in 2006. Photo: Vincent Baumgartner

9

THE RUSSIANS ARE COMING

Horst learned the hard way that humankind is more resilient than we give ourselves credit for. Since his experience of the Holocaust, he has felt that just at the moment when you think you can't take it anymore, you may be surprised to find out how tough you really are. Such was the case in his own life. It was during this time, when the weaker ones had already succumbed to their fate, the strongest forged on and the Russian army came to a standstill on the outskirts of Budapest. The bombing of the city had been going on for quite some time and rumor spread that the Russians tried to miss the Ghetto in the process but once in a while they miscalculated and not only did some shells hit the Ghetto, people were killed by them.

In a time when so many were sent to concentration camps or killed, one young man in Horst's building managed to survive many horrors in the previous two years. After he was picked up off the streets of Hungary and sent to Russia to be used as slave labor, he made it back to the Ghetto with hardly a scratch. Then one day, while ascending the stairs of his apartment building, a shell hit the staircase above him. A piece of shrapnel from the shell sheared off his arm at the elbow. Fortunately, a doctor got there in time and the young fellow lived.

As the bombings intensified, those who were able to, moved down into the cellar to live, which really meant just sitting in a chair all day, every day. Together, they persevered. More people died sitting in those chairs. The cellar was shrouded in darkness and electricity worked only sporadically, leaving little differentiation between day and night. Time no longer mattered to them as day blurred into night in the darkness. Day after day and night after night, Selma sat in that cellar without complaint. She wasn't the only one who had to endure hardships, but she was the oldest in the house to survive.

To add to the fear and anxiety that shrouded them throughout those dark hours, every day the Nylos went into the cellars and picked any man they thought was fit enough and inducted him into rubble control, cleaning the mess above ground. None of these laborers ever returned. Later, Horst learned that during the final months of the war, the Nazis picked 20,000 Jews from the Ghetto, forced them to work and then walked them to the Danube River. They had them stand at the edge of the water and with their machine guns killed every last one of them. Those who didn't fall directly into the water were thrown in. The Danube River ran red for quite a while as the Nazis kept returning to the cellar just to scare the inhabitants. (Stern, 2006)

Male workers weren't the only victims of this mass execution. Today, 60 pairs of shoes sit on the bank of the Danube River, designed from metal to look like those of the period. The monument is called "The Shoes on the Danube Promenade." It is a poignant tribute to not only the men but also the women and children who were so viciously murdered there during the 1944-1945 winter, by the militiamen of the Arrow Cross Party.

The Shoes on the Danube Promenade, 2009 Budapest. Photo: Public Domain

Although the Nazis searched the cellars daily for extra help, with each visit, they passed up the opportunity to recruit Horst. This was certainly out of the ordinary. Few young men went unscathed during this ordeal and his mother knew this. He was spared this time because Erna had been clever.

When they were first reunited and he entered the Ghetto, Erna saw how skinny Horst was, weighing no more than 75 pounds. He had a smooth face and long hair, so she made him wear a pair of women's pants, a pullover sweater, and a scarf on his head, which tied under his chin. In doing so, he passed as a girl, albeit not an attractive one. He quips now that, "I saw myself in a mirror once, and even I would have refused a date with myself."

Thinking ahead, Erna had introduced him, right from the start, as her daughter Kathy. Disguised as a skinny, dirty, young girl, who smelled awful, Horst was able to avoid conscription. No one ever questioned him and the only people who were aware of his true identity was the person with whom he had broken into the cabinet and his wife. Erna's plan worked until the end.

After the war ended, Horst would walk down the street with

Erna and occasionally meet up with other survivors. They looked at him and turned to Erna and asked whatever happened to her daughter Kathy. Erna would tell them that he was Kathy. They looked at him in disbelief and walked on.

Peeking out the front door of the apartment house one day, Horst saw a huge German tank rattling down the street, with its cannon blazing in the direction from where the Russians were supposed to be advancing. The next day, he saw the same action taking place in reverse, only this time it was the Russians who were advancing. Not long after having left his observation post, some other boys were killed in the crossfire while standing in the same spot that he had vacated earlier. Horst was shaken to think of how easily that might have been him. How sad that they had come this far, unharmed, only to end up getting killed at the very end of the war. Not long after that incident, the war was over for all of them.

On January 18, 1945, after 12 long and miserable years, the war had finally ended for Horst and his family. Intense shooting was followed by sudden quiet. Before they really understood the significance of what had just happened, they heard footsteps coming down the cellar steps and then there stood about six wild looking soldiers, one of whom spoke in a language that none of them recognized: Russian.

The remaining residents of the cellar (six, including the Sterns) sat there, terrified, until another Russian soldier arrived and spoke to them in Hungarian. He informed them that they were free and recommended they return to their pre-ghetto homes to see if their former lives could be resumed. That was a nice thought, but how could anything ever be the same? Was there even anything left to return to if they tried? The very idea of freedom seemed foreign and it was one that was difficult to trust. They went upstairs to stretch out and rest.

Horst awoke before the others, so he quietly ventured out to the street to have a look around. Dead bodies littered the street and gutters, most of whom died as a result of their curiosity. Unfortunately, they chose to investigate the source of the shooting and ultimately ended up in the crossfire while the fighting was still going on. The sight of so many corpses had little impact on anyone. The sad reality was that they had all become desensitized to the sight after so many years surrounded by death.

Horst's focus shifted from the still, lifeless forms before him to movement in the streets. People appeared from every nook and cranny, walking with their arms full of food and other merchandise. At precisely that moment, he realized the full impact of what freedom meant. This was the moment that he and his family had dreamed of for years. He, his mother, and his grandmother had survived the ghetto in Budapest. They had, in fact, defied the almost certain death sentence that came with being a Jew living in the shadow of the Danube River. Now they had the freedom to act according to their own will and to take charge of their own lives for the first time in years. A daunting realization.

10

THE AFTERMATH

The first group of Russian soldiers didn't stay long, staying only long enough to fight their way through, then they were replaced by the occupation forces. The first week was a time of retribution. Most of the higher-ranking Nazis were able to get out and evade justice, but some of them were caught, mostly locals. Horst explains,

"Justice was fast in those days. Once caught, they were judged and found guilty on the spot and subsequently hung from the nearest lamppost. It was quite a sight to behold. My personal opinion is that they died too easily, considering all the suffering they had caused." (Stern, 2006)

Obtaining free groceries was easy thanks to the Russians. It was them who broke the locks and smashed the glass of the storefronts. They helped themselves to alcohol and anything of value and left the rest to the residents. Even though there was enough for everyone, it wasn't uncommon for people to fight over the food. It took some time for them to learn to act as members of the human race again rather than rely on their animal instincts, that had thus far kept them alive during the war. Horst quickly grabbed whatever he could until his hands and pockets were full.

Although he had difficulty getting out of the store, once out of the mob action, he took advantage of his speed and ran as fast as his feet would carry him toward home. His stash included a large jar of marmalade, chocolate, sugar, and some cookies. Both Erna and Selma's faces registered a degree of shock unseen by Horst previously as he produced his ill-gotten goods. Naturally, his mother questioned him, demanding to know where all of it had come from. His reply? "The same place everyone else got theirs." That seemed to satisfy his elders, and they began to eat.

Once they finished their feast, Horst told them that he should go back out and see what other food might "need to be liberated" since he didn't think that the stores would reopen for a while. They decided it would be best for the two ladies to stay at home and guard the first stash. Horst quickly found another store and once again awaited the departure of the Russian soldiers who were inside. Had he followed immediately and gotten in the soldiers' way, there was a chance of getting shot, so he waited his turn patiently. Once they found their liquor and moved out, Horst set about on his mission to retrieve all things edible.

By day three, their supply had grown tremendously and even included non-edible items such as sewing needles, yarn, shaving soap, blankets, pillows, and sheets. These items later became their currency as they bartered for food. Liberation, unfortunately, didn't mean their living conditions magically improved. People were still starving, and desperation was still evident. Horst came upon a group of people dissecting a dead horse in the street. He accepted a piece of the meat, which he brought home to his grandmother, and didn't disclose its origins. She made a stew with the unidentified meat and some of the spices that he had found earlier, and they shared it with friends who miraculously produced carrots and potatoes to add to it. No one asked questions.

On the fourth day following liberation, Horst, Selma, and Erna felt well enough to leave the apartment and move back to the place they had lived before. There they discovered that the lady that had owned the apartment didn't survive, but most of the young ladies-of-the-night that she had rented to before returned as well. There was no problem with Horst's family returning. Some of the ladies had escaped capture by the Nazis because they weren't Jewish. All of the others were fortunate enough to make it back in one piece, and quickly resumed their lives.

There was little left in the room they had once occupied, only a bed, chest of drawers, a table, and a few chairs, but the most important part of the room remained. There, in all of its glory, was the potbellied stove. People from other apartments on the floor began to return some of the items that Erna had been forced to leave behind. They were grateful for the return of sheets, pots, pans, and towels that had been safeguarded by neighbors in their absence.

Once they settled back into their apartment, Horst returned to the streets to find more food. He recalls that, "Budapest was an open city, and it was every man for himself." Yet, even in the absence of police, there was hardly any crime to speak of. People seemed to realize that they were all in the same situation and were just happy to have survived. The hard times they had all endured definitely brought out the best in people. Horst continued to "organize," as he called it, a nicer way of referring to stealing food.

Sometimes luck was with him, like the day he passed a butcher shop. At first, he looked through the broken window and it appeared that almost everything had already been taken. Yet, something told him to investigate further. He moved some empty boxes around and discovered a door that led to a cellar. The window above the door let in just enough light to illuminate several boxes full of lard. He could only carry two at a time and tried to hide the rest until he could return but by the time he got back, the rest had disappeared. He could only assume that someone had seen him leave. He managed to get a slab of bacon, flour, and some sugar though.

A few days later, he once again found fortune. They were in constant need of materials to burn in their stove and as he walked down the street he came upon the coffee shop two doors down. This shop sold coffee beans from all over the world. He noticed that this shop had also been emptied by looters. Entering the store anyway, he once again found a cellar door. There, he found a 50-

pound bag of potatoes and all the coal briquettes he could want. He was able to "liberate" all the potatoes and made three or four trips for the coal before he was once again observed and someone else finished the job. The coal he was able to get home ended up being a lifesaver during the cold winter of 1945.

Just as things started to look better, Erna and Selma contracted Dysentery. Hospitals, doctors, and medicines were luxuries that weren't available to them so Horst acted as nursemaid to both of them. He provided hot soups and whatever care he could, and eventually, both recovered. Fortunately, despite all three of them sharing a bed, with Horst at the foot of it with a chair on the side for his own feet, just like when they were in the ghetto, he didn't catch the illness.

During this time, Horst had to have a wisdom tooth pulled out. He found a dentist in the neighborhood who was willing to pull the tooth for the price of eight potatoes, with the stipulation that, because he didn't have Novocain, or any other painkiller, he would use four friends of his to hold Horst down. There was one person for each arm, for each leg, and a belt around his midriff. The procedure worked, but he can still feel the sensation of that tooth being pulled out to this day.

11

BARTER AND TRADE

Once again, the food supply started running low. Horst decided that the only way to replenish it would be to take some of the stuff he had so carefully organized to the nearest farm or town where he might be able to exchange some of it for some food. The nearest farm from Budapest was about 25 kilometers away and took about a day for Horst to reach as he wasn't in optimal health yet.

It was late afternoon when Horst walked up to the farmhouse and knocked on the door, which was opened almost at once, and he was quickly invited in. Horst showed the owner razor blades, knitting needles, knitting yarn, sewing material, and a few other things. The bartering was successful. By the time they had finished it was dark so the farmer kindly offered Horst lodging for the night and fed him a memorable meal. The next morning, following a good night's sleep and a good breakfast, he picked up his belongings and hurried back to Budapest.

On Horst's first trip, his bartering system worked very well. The farmer exchanged the food that he produced for items that he couldn't produce himself. However, when he returned three days later to try again, the farmer apologized and said that he couldn't help him this time. He also informed Horst that since he had left him the last time, there must have been at least 20 others just like him trying to exchange their meager goods for anything edible. So, he continued on further away from the city until he finally came to a farmhouse no one else had been to yet. This generous farmer filled his backpack with potatoes, flour, some ham, bacon, and he even put some eggs into a bag for him to take as well.

He turned around and hiked back into the city that same night, even though he had walked for most of the day. Visualizing the moment when he could climb the stairs, knock on the window, and hand over all of the food to Erna and Selma motivated him to keep moving. He knew he couldn't risk going through the rooms of sleeping people. If they woke up, they would see his stash of food. All the walking and bartering was worth it when he saw the look on Erna and Selma's faces, they lit up at the sight of what he had brought home. He quickly climbed through the window to join them.

After eating the ham and eggs Selma fixed them for breakfast, Horst went to bed and slept for the next eight hours. He reflects, "You cannot imagine how an egg tastes after you haven't had one for such a long time, in two words, absolutely delicious." The meal inspired him to make the trip twice a week. He began within a 50-kilometer radius but soon had to extend it as the competition was great. His trips weren't always successful, but he always brought something back with him and he never met a farmer who wouldn't at least talk to him. If they couldn't help him, they often led him to others who might be able to barter with him. Although most of his trips were daytrips, they would often offer to put him up for the night and feed him meals during his stay.

Securing food wasn't the only problem for Horst and his family, in those early days after the ghetto. Lice plagued them all. They all had them, in their hair and in their clothes. Horst had to shave his head for relief, but they still remained in the clothing. What made matters worse was that water for washing was hard to come by. There was a fire hydrant a block and a half away. Horst would have to stand in line to get water, fill up whatever container he had, and then carry it up four flights of stairs. He would repeat this process over and over again, filling every container he could find.

Stores were still closed, with the exception of one little entrepreneur here or there trying to sell some cloth, or a few books, but everybody was looking for food. It would take at least another month or so before that happened. As time passed, the distance that Horst had to walk to find farmers willing to barter for food continued to increase and before long, it required a three-day walk. This meant camping outside, and in the month of February, that meant bitter cold. He survived these conditions but came across others who didn't.

After one such trip, from which Horst didn't have much to show, he figured that was the end of it; if the stores didn't open soon, with some kind of food for sale, more people would die from hunger. They had already lost so many, mostly the elderly or the very young, some of whom had just given up on life and frozen to death in their apartments. Many weren't found until summer.

Fortunately, soon after Horst's musings on the desperate need for open markets, the bakery around the corner, the one where Erna had been picked up from not that long before, reopened. Before long, they were standing in line with all the others, hoping that by the time their turn came, there would still be some bread left. It was a start in the right direction and one that was long overdue.

Rumors began circulating that the trains were running again. Upon hearing this, Horst was immediately reminded of a train he had seen during his ordeal. Running through the center of town on the streetcar tracks, the train carried boxcar after boxcar, each filled to the top with corpses of people collected off the streets after the fighting had stopped and also of those who had been buried temporarily in parks all over the city.

"*There were men, women, and children of all ages. All created equal even in death. I am pretty sure that the ones we had heaved over the wall were amongst them. The ones who had died in our house was surely amongst them. There must have been thousands of them. One stacked on top of the other. Their bodies had swollen grotesquely like balloons and the flesh turned the colors of the rainbow. It was a sight, never to be forgotten. I won't even mention the stink they emitted even though it was in the middle of winter."* (Stern, 2006)

The rumors were substantiated. The trains were in fact, finally, running again from the Teleki Train Station in Pest. However, with no timetable, service was unreliable at best. Potential passengers took their chances on where the train was going or when the train would finally depart. Some didn't have to wait too long but others waited for days, hoping to get on the right train for their desired destination, and even then, they couldn't count on getting there. They often ended up going in the opposite direction.

First, there was a mass of people trying to get off the train, those who had waited on it for a couple of days only to find out that it wasn't going to where they wanted to go to. According to Horst, you really had to be there and see it to believe it. Masses of people fought to get on the train. One family member would get on, rush to the nearest window, and try to pull the rest of the family into the train through the window.

Horst soon realized that he had little chance of getting onto the train. Before long, even the roof of the train was filled with people. The only place that wasn't occupied were the bumpers of the train cars. Horst threw the blanket that he always carried with him over the bumper, straddled it as if mounting a horse and hoped for the best.

Horst was a little nervous as the train started to move because he didn't know what to expect but other than a few bumps whenever the train operator had to apply the brakes, it went pretty smoothly. Unfortunately, a few people who took the chance to ride on the roof fell off and didn't survive. Although not wise, Horst continued to take his chances on the bumper.

As Horst perfected his bumper-riding technique, he risked two extended shopping trips and rode the bumper every time. In retrospect, he realizes how stupid the risk was and how lucky he is to have survived. He enjoyed having the company of the man who often rode the other bumper, so he could have someone to talk to. The man lived in another part of the country, he talked of how he had been enrolled into the army and how he was lucky not to have been sent to the Russian front. He also spoke of being a cook, but Horst admits that at the time, he couldn't have cared less. The conversation helped pass the time and the miles. He had no idea where he would depart the train.

Unfortunately, traveling this way still involved risk. At any time, the Russian Army would stop one of the trains and commandeer the locomotive for an indefinite period of time. It happened to Horst twice. On each occasion, another train was eventually sent for them. The first time it was six hours before the locomotive was returned, and the second time, it was an all-night affair.

The first time it happened, Horst got off the train, and walked for about an hour until he arrived at a farmhouse. Horst knocked on the door and asked the man if he was open to bartering. The farmer hadn't seen anyone for a very long time, so he was happy to barter, and supplied him with quite a large supply of food. He stayed the night then backtracked the way he had come the previous day. Finally reaching the train tracks, he began his wait. He was fortunate enough to have only a three-hour wait before a slow-moving train approached. He had strategically positioned himself at a sharp turn in the track, so the train slowed down enough for him to mount one of the bumpers. He made it home in record time and was only gone a little over three days.

Running out of merchandise to bargain with, Horst knew his travelling days were coming to an end. His last railroad trip occurred a week later and lasted for over a week. The trip there was moderately successful, taking three days to get there on the same locomotive. He ended up with the usual things, some vegetables, some flour, lard, a small slab of bacon, and best of all, a live chicken.

However, Horst wasn't as fortunate on the return trip. Although it started out well, the Russian army, once again, decided to borrow the train on which he was traveling. The unexpected hiatus lasted longer than a few hours this time, though. Instead, he faced a couple of days in snow-covered fields. As night settled in, cooking fires began to pop up all along the railway line. After searching the nearby woods, he too had gathered items needed for a fire of his own. Soon, a couple of men came along and asked to share his fire. The three combined some of their food stores and made a soup.

Henry reminisces about the live chicken on this journey. He wrapped a string around its leg so it wouldn't run away and as the men ate soup, he fed the chicken some breadcrumbs. He developed an interesting friendship with that chicken, and he gave it the name that was used for him in the ghetto; Kathy.

After the three men had eaten, they listened for any kind of train noise coming from the tracks. They figured that it would be a long night, so they decided to bed down for a while.

As one day led into another, tempers began to flare. Hundreds of people were frustrated about being stranded during the middle of winter and under circumstances that none of them could control. They didn't even know how far they were from Budapest, not that it really mattered. Following another night, at about ten in the morning, all heads went up listening to the noise of the locomotive coming closer and closer. It was music to their ears and they all piled back onto the train. Kathy and Horst rode the bumper. Kathy either sat on his lap or she would sit on his shoulder. He remembers now that it was amazing how much warmth that chicken generated.

Horst and his new pet finally arrived in Budapest in the early evening and sheer exhaustion led him straight to bed where he slept, almost around the clock. Waking up once, he saw a vision of Kathy sitting on the iron bed board staring at him.

"I never got a cluck out of her before, but when I called her name she hopped onto the bed and greeted me like a long-lost friend. Whoever said that chickens have no soul? I got rather attached to that little bugger. Is that what people mean by bonding?" (Stern, 2006)

Unfortunately, his mother saw it from a different perspective and the next time he woke up, Kathy was gone and the aroma of delicious chicken soup filled the room. When he confronted his mother about how she could cook the only friend he had on his last journey, Erna replied that the chicken sacrificed herself and gave up her life so that they could live and have a good meal. He saw the logic in her statement and after eating his fill, felt like a cannibal who had just eaten his best friend.

He felt somewhat better after his grandmother spent a few hours heating up water for a bath. As soon as he slipped into the water, he thought he had struck gold. He says it wasn't quite that good in actuality but it felt good to be clean again and he eventually forgave himself for eating Kathy.

12

THE NEW BEGINNING

Horst turned 17 in April of 1945 and winter was still hanging on. He, his mother, and grandmother had somehow managed to survive and had even managed to gain some weight but they needed to figure out what to do next. The open city status had been revoked, and things started to get back to normal. Police were back on the streets again, making residents feel a bit safer walking at night. More stores reopened and Horst sold some of the larger items he had "organized." Among the items was an expensive German Leica camera and some new clothing. The money these high-ticket items brought supported them for a little while longer.

Horst knew that he had to start earning a steady income to help support his family, so his next venture involved starting a little business with the help of a friend of Erna and his Uncle Robert. Siegbert had survived the war by hiding with a gentile friend. Horst remembers that, before the war, he was in the business of importing pearls and he had some good connections in Switzerland, from where he now imported watches and gold-plated watchbands.

Siegbert came up with the idea to give Horst enough credit to start selling items and then Horst would pay him back as soon as he had sold them. Horst set up his "storefront" in Andrassi Utca, a popular business district. His store consisted of a large food tray with handles, on which he had threaded a string through the handles long enough to go around his neck. He jokes that his storefront had low overheads and that the junior entrepreneur was in business.

After putting about a dozen watchbands on his tray, he didn't have to wait long before they were sold out. The Russian soldiers were his best, and actually, his only customers. At first, he worried that one of them would pick up all of the watchbands up and simply walk away. There wouldn't have been anything he could have done about it, had that happened.

As a poorly dressed, skinny kid who had yet the need to shave, Horst didn't appear as the tough salesman type and that appearance is what he believes helped him to succeed. He had taken off his Star of David by then but its outline was still recognizable on his coat. He had no trouble at all though and boasts that he "made out like a bandit." He had anticipated that communication would be poor, at best, and so he was prepared with pencil and paper, anytime he was asked how much, all he had to do was write down the price, and the deal was complete. It was a pleasure for Horst to deal with those soldiers because there was no haggling whatsoever. He had about four different styles of watchbands to choose from and once they saw the price, they pulled out a wad of money and usually rounded up the price for Horst. To him, the soldiers seemed fascinated with watches, and he says, "It was not an unusual sight to see a soldier with both of his arms strapped full, from his wrist to his elbows with watches."

Horst made some interesting observations about those Russian soldiers. Of particular interest was how they went out of their way to be nice to children. They spoiled them by giving them candy and toys they had liberated from stores and even played with them in the street. He found it odd to see those fierce looking men in uniforms, with their rifles slung over their shoulder taking a kid for a bicycle ride, and when finished, giving the bike to the kid. It made him think that on some level, all of us must possess a gentle side within us.

One day, while walking on the street, Erna and Horst ran into their friends and former roommates from the ghetto. He can't remember their names, so he refers to them as Mr. and Mrs. Pancake, due to their joint cooking experiments. Before they all ended up in the ghetto, Mr. Pancake used to own and run his own little factory, not far from where they lived. He went back into business manufacturing custom jewelry.

After catching up, he invited Horst to witness a public hanging. A man and a woman had been tried and convicted in court for murdering Jews during the last days of the war. He offered for Horst to meet him at the jailhouse where the hanging was going to take place. Horst told him that he would "love to see those vermin hung."

Erna chose not to attend and explained that she had to go somewhere with her mother but Horst was there at the appointed time, met Mr. Pancake, and they both went into the courtyard where the hanging would take place at six o'clock in the morning. Two guards brought out the male prisoner promptly at six o'clock. Hands bound behind his back, he looked to be no more than 30 years old. He was escorted to a nearby table. The man sitting behind it looked up at the prisoner and read from a folder. He declared to the prisoner that he had been found guilty of war crimes against humanity and he would be hanged by the neck until pronounced dead. In his most direct manner, Horst explained how this hanging was handled in a different way.

"I have seen them [people] hung from a light pole up high. A noose around their neck and a couple of guys to pull the condemned man up, and all you had to do was to watch them dance a little, no music. Now, this so-called hanging was different in the sense that there was no light pole. Or a tree branch to throw a rope over, not even old-fashioned gallows where the condemned man stood on a trap door, and the executioner waiting for the sign, to release the trap door.

This one was more like a garroting, done with a rope. There was just a 12-foot four by four post buried into the ground. A big spike was driven into the four by four post, about 12 inches above the ground. There was a small stool that stood about ten inches high, that the prisoner was told to stand on. Once he stood there, he was asked, if there was anything that he wanted to say? Shaking his head, one of the guards put a sack over the condemned man's head, positioned the rope around his neck, and took position behind the pole on a stepladder. Then he took hold of the rope that was around the prisoner's neck and wound the rope around another big spike that was driven in on top of the four by four pole and secured it there.

Next, the guard who stood in front, yanked the stool from under the man's feet who then dropped a few inches. In order to hasten his death, the guard on top took hold of the prisoner's head, one hand under the chin, and the other hand resting on top of the man's head and he started to twist, trying to break his neck, while the guard in front who had tied the prisoners feet, left enough rope so he could wind it under the spike, and started to pull. It was not the best way to hang a man, but then I have never met anyone who could convince me that there was a good hanging.

During the whole procedure no one spoke, all was quiet while everybody watched. There must have been at least a hundred people watching, and interestingly, 80 percent of them were women. It took him a long time to die. After about ten minutes, the attending physician pronounced the prisoner dead.

After that announcement people cheered for a while, till a side door opened, and they brought out the woman prisoner. It was the same routine as before. She died the same way. Nice and slow. Remember that all those people who were watching had lost loved ones to those monsters." (Stern, 2006)

The very matter-of-fact way in which Horst relays stories such as this today, further confirms that survivors of the Holocaust have various coping mechanisms. While some continue to live traumatized by all they have seen, others, like Horst, have formed thick skins and can relay their accounts in a forthright detached manner and even, almost unbelievably, at times with a sense of humor. With all they have seen and experienced, situations that both you and I could probably never imagine, I respect all of them for the many ways they have found to live with that they have endured.

Horst felt that he had seen justice done that day, especially considering that most of the people responsible for the heinous crimes committed during the Holocaust got away with their crimes and never had to pay for them in any way.

13

A NEW CAREER

After Horst had been in business for about a month or so, Erna had a talk with him. It seemed that as his mother, she wanted more for her son than his little sales-tray business. As they spoke of his future, Erna came up with the idea that it might be good for Horst to learn a trade. He was reminded of how much he had enjoyed working in the goldsmith shop prior to the war and thought that might be the right trade for him.

Horst and his mother returned to the shop to find no one there. They found the superintendent of the building and inquired about what had happened to the business and the people who had run it. They learned that only one young man made it back. The others never returned from Russia where they had been deported to and where they had died as slave laborers. The owner of the business perished in Auschwitz like so many others.

Following the disappointment of the goldsmith shop, Horst thought to look up their friends from the ghetto and find out more about what Mr. Pancake manufactured at his business. When they had last run into him, he had given them the location and as it turned out, it was located on a little side street only a ten-minute walk from home.

Mr. and Mrs. Pancake were happy to see Horst and Erna again.

They explained that when the couple returned to the store after leaving the ghetto, they found it looted just like all the other stores but at least his machinery was mostly intact and he was able to reestablish a connection with his supplier.

Horst asked him if he could use an apprentice. He explained to the man that he had worked, for a very short time, in a goldsmith shop. The man replied that he would be happy to put Horst on the payroll but he wouldn't be able to pay much because business had just started. The man was anxious to have him there and to see how things would work out with Horst as his apprentice. He began working within a week. It differed from the previous shop in that they didn't produce individual pieces of jewelry but mass-produced pieces instead, but they weren't bad looking.

As the city of Budapest got back on its feet, the stores continued to reopen, and the newspapers tried to build excitement by convincing the residents of how great everything would soon be. They encouraged cooperation with the government and implored people to follow the new laws as they were introduced. Erna took over Horst's little "store front" business, adding some custom-made jewelry from the store where he worked. Erna talked Siegbert into importing some cheaper watches from Switzerland. Then she sold them to stores in Budapest.

Erna was making fairly decent money and was smart enough to exchange some into dollars on the black market and for the first time since arriving in Hungary, the family finally had enough food and clothing. They finally began to look healthy. He found out years later, when he got an x-ray for his emigration to Canada, that he had contacted tuberculosis during his ordeal and it had left him with a small hole in his lung, which healed itself when he started eating a healthy diet.

Although change would soon come, for the moment Horst and Erna decided to try to improve their business once again. Erna would buy as much merchandise in the morning as she could get. There still wasn't much to be had, food was still the best commodity because the population was still hungry. Therefore, the items they were looking for were strictly for the Russian forces that occupied Budapest, but they kept seeing fewer and fewer of them.

Erna continued to do fine for a while. She bought in the morning and sold out within a few days, but as soon as her merchandise sold out and she tried to restock, she was quoted a higher price than she had sold the last lot for. Inflation was staring them in the face, but they still ignored it.

Horst doesn't remember who provided the information, but someone informed his mother that she would be able to buy all the custom jewelry she would need in Vienna, Austria. It was the hub for custom jewelry manufacturing in Europe. She had no names or addresses of the manufacturers but decided to risk a trip and she convinced her son to take time off from work to go along with her.

Convincing Horst to make the trip wasn't difficult. Disenchanted with life after being in a prison for seven long years, as he puts it, he really had nothing to lose by taking the risk. He had escaped actual incarceration in a concentration camp but had been hunted for each of those years. He wasn't pursued for anything he had done wrong or even for his political views but simply because he was Jewish. He couldn't see a future for himself in Hungary and even entertained the idea of just packing up and seeing the world, but with his mother and grandmother there, he just couldn't leave them on their own, and his moral obligation to them outweighed the desire to leave, so they had to find a way to make their business work to provide the necessities for survival.

In retrospect, Horst attributes all the problems of those war years and deprivation for affecting their reasoning and common sense, but they decided to go on the buying trip to Austria. It never occurred to them that with inflation all around them, even if they came back with suitcases full of merchandise, people might not have the money to buy. Even if they sold enough merchandise and tripled their investment, they still would have gone broke. Besides, in going to Austria, they would have to cross the border twice, once going and once coming back. His excuse for this poor decision was that he was too young to take all those risks into consideration.

Upon arriving at the train station to get their tickets to Vienna, the ticket seller quoted them a price far above the amount of money they had brought with them, so they decided to postpone their trip until the next day. In order to finance this trip, they had to go to Horst's grandmother because she was the keeper of all of the family funds. They told her their plan and all she had to say was, "Don't forget to come back." They assured her that they would return and they made arrangements with neighbors to look in and make sure that she was all right. They figured they'd be gone for no more than five days.

Erna and Horst returned to the station the next morning and despite the fact that the ticket prices had increased yet again, they purchased their tickets. At that time, they had no way of knowing what was in store for them. Interestingly though, the crazy decision to go to Austria was going to change the direction of their lives. The plan was to make the trip there in one day, spend three days buying the merchandise they needed, and then take one day for the return trip. Only, it didn't quite work out that way.

How Horst and Erna didn't end up in jail remains a mystery. First of all, they didn't have passports. All Erna had was her birth certificate and a written piece of paper with Horst's name and several official-looking stamps on it. The train halted at the border and in walked two border guards who then asked for passports and tickets from everyone aboard.

When the time came to show their passports, they told them that they had the train tickets but no passports. The guard asked them to follow him. They got off the train and followed him to a building where they entered a small room where another man in uniform waited. The guard whispered to the man at the desk, most likely telling him that they didn't have passports. The man looked at them and wanted to know what they were doing on that train without any papers.

Anticipating some kind of trouble, Erna and Horst had rehearsed their stories beforehand, and so they told him that they were German Jews, born in Berlin. That said they escaped Germany in 1940 and lived illegally for all those years with a kind, gentile, family who had made it their business to save Jews from the

Nazis. All this went on with both of them speaking in German, which was their native language, and the little of Hungarian they had picked up while they lived in hiding wasn't fluent enough to cause them any problems.

Their charade worked. The border guards wished them good luck, escorted them back to the train, and they continued their journey. It wasn't until midnight that they finally pulled into the train station on the outskirts of Vienna. They had finally reached Austria.

14

VIENNA

The winds blew cold on the January night that Horst and Erna arrived in Vienna-Neustadt, a suburb of Vienna. The train station was quite far from the inner city, where they were told they would be able to find what they were looking for. Streetcars stopped running hours prior to their arrival. When they asked someone if there was a hotel nearby the person looked at them as if they were crazy. So, they started walking towards the general direction of the inner city.

Walking down the snow-covered, deserted, streets brought a sense of eeriness, despite the surrounding beauty. It was just the two of them, not a car in sight. In this unsettling and desolate setting, Erna and Horst began to realize, for the first time, the devastation the war had left behind. Entire blocks of houses that had once stood were now gone, victims of the bombardment by the American Air Force.

After walking for about half an hour, they finally saw a light in the distance, which turned out to be a police station, for which they were grateful, as this was the first place Horst and his mother had come across in the last hour. They were relieved to make human contact and figured that they might finally be directed to a hotel where they could spend the night. However, after talking to a policeman and telling him what they were looking for, he told them that there was no accommodation like that available. It would take some time before everything went back to normal.

The best thing the officer could offer them was a room with a couple of mattresses and blankets on the floor. He got them situated and then departed. Exhaustion overtook them and they were asleep as soon as they closed their eyes.

Awakened by the smell of coffee, Horst and his mother arose and freshened up the best they could. Then, they accepted the officer's invitation to sit at his desk where there were fresh rolls and jam waiting for them. The officer asked them what brought them there, in the middle of the night.

Erna told him the same story she had told the border guard at the border crossing. Afterward, she just couldn't resist the temptation of saying,

"*If this happened 12 months ago, instead of sleeping on the floor, we would have, most likely, ended up in a cell for the night and instead of a breakfast, the Gestapo would have picked us up in the morning.*" The man didn't know what to say, so Erna said, "*Thank goodness the war is over. Too many people have been killed on all sides. It will take some time for the wounds to heal, but that is what time does best.*" (Stern, 2006)

To Horst's surprise, the officer then told them that if they were serious about getting back to Berlin, he might be able to help. He gave them an address to go to in Vienna; it was the Robert Koch Hospital where an organization called the UNRRA (United Nation Relief and Rehabilitation Agency) was located. This group specialized in the repatriation of people who were persecuted because of their religion.

Following breakfast, the policeman escorted them to the streetcar stop, and when the tram arrived, he told the conductor to make sure that we reached our destination. He wished us well as he paid the fare for us.

After a while, the conductor came around to tell Erna and Horst that the next stop was the Robert Koch Hospital. They decided to see what this UNRRA was all about. They walked into the building and up to the registration window, where they were asked their names and told to sit down. They were assured that someone would be with them momentarily. Not too long after, they were called into an office. A man in an American uniform got up from behind his desk and introduced himself. Speaking in perfect German, he asked them how he might help them.

He told them that he was working for the UNRRA headquartered in Vienna, which was set up after the end of the war. He explained that their goal was to try help survivors get back to their homes or to immigrate to a country of their choice.

Erna told him how they had travelled to Vienna and the reason for their journey. He looked at them as if they had lost their minds. He then explained that there were dozens and dozens of DP (displaced persons) camps located all over Germany, for people with problems just like ours. He asked if they would be interested in that type of a set up and invited them to stay for a few days to think it over. He asked them to let him know their decision when they were ready.

After being led into a big room, with its walls lined with army cots, they were told to pick a couple and that lunch would be served at noon in the dining hall. Horst recalls:

"There were people of all ages there. At least a dozen languages were spoken, all at the same time, including Yiddish, which is a German dialect. We learned that this place was a collecting station and transports were formed here and that the people would eventually wind up in one of the many DP camps in Germany. We realized that this was a once in a lifetime opportunity and would change our lives for the better." (Stern, 2006)

They made an appointment at the front office to talk with an officer and soon the same gentleman that they had spoken with originally explained that he could have them on a transport to a DP camp in Germany within a few days. That's when Erna told him that they were happy to take him up on his offer but there was a slight issue that they had to take care of first. She told him that they had left her mother, who was almost 80 years old, in Budapest and that they would need to pick her up. They couldn't return to Germany without her.

The officer seemed quite surprised and told them this was the first time he encountered an elderly Jewish woman who had survived the Nazis. However, he explained that there was nothing he could do to help get Selma out of Budapest. He promised that if they could find a way to get her to Vienna, he would be able to help them. He also advised that they see the Jewish Organization in Budapest because they had ways to get people out of Hungary. He cautioned that the Russians had started to tighten up their borders, so it wasn't going to be easy.

15

SAVING SELMA

Following an early breakfast (which incidentally turned out to be their only meal for the day), they walked to the train station. Upon inquiring, they discovered that there was a train departing for Budapest in the early afternoon. They showed their return tickets but were told that they were now invalid due to the chaotic situation in Hungary. In fact, they learned that the Hungarian currency, the Pengo, was worthless on the market and that they had to pay for their fare in Austrian currency. Fortunately, they had enough Austrian money to cover their fare. Horst thought, *bless my grandmother for handing us our savings before we started this foolish journey.*

The train left the station on time and before Horst and his mother knew it, they were at the Hungarian border again. They were surprised to see how much things had changed in the few days since they had crossed the border. Most notably were the several Russians soldiers on the train. They approached the Sterns and asked to see identification. Erna told him the same story she had used coming into Austria. Only this time she did so in fluent Hungarian. She spoke of coming back home after being picked up by the Nazis and sent to Germany as slave laborers. She claimed that the only thing they wanted now was to go home and see if any of their extended family was still alive. Once again, the story worked. One could only imagine what might have happened to the pair had no one believed them.

Arriving home, they discovered that Horst's grandmother was fine and the people in the house had taken good care of her while they were gone. Outside the building though, things weren't as good. Once they reached the market the next day, they were shocked to discover that most of the store shelves were almost empty. Horst wondered how everything could change so much in just one week. Business had come to a near standstill. Inflation jumped so rapidly that prices increased from 100 Pengos, to 1,000 Pengos, to 10,000 Pengos, and then to 100,000 Pengos (The Pengo was the official name for the Hungarian currency at the time but has since changed. In fact, postwar Hungary suffered the worst documented hyperinflation in history. The government decided that in order to stem this inflation, they would devalue all paper currency and print new money and although it was still called the Pengo, the denominations changed. Basically, they started all over again.) (Stern, 2006)

Meanwhile, Selma was relieved and happy for Erna and Horst's return. They shared the account of everything that had happened to them with her. When they told her about the DP camps in Germany and the possibility they offered for immigration to the United States, she said that it would be a good chance for Horst to make something of himself. She was in complete agreement to leave Budapest as soon as possible and since none of them could see much of a future in Hungary, the decision was easily made.

After reaching the conclusion that change would be for the best, the next day they went to the Jewish Organization to see if they could help them to get out of Hungary. As it turned out, their timing was just right. The people who were putting together another transport were a few travelers short but were sure that they could fill the vacant spots within a few days with Horst and his family. They told Horst's family that if they wanted to go that the plan was to leave within five days but they couldn't take more than two suitcases per person.

All three of them were registered by name, Erna Stern, Horst Stern, and Selma Stern, but the man documenting the trio looked up and questioned why he only saw Erna and Horst.

Erna explained that they had left her mother at home because she was elderly and they had hoped to spare her the walk. As very few people of Selma's age had survived the war, the man wasn't easily convinced but eventually relented and registered all three of them.

To the delight of the Sterns, everything happened very quickly. When they returned home from registering for the trip and gave the news to Horst's grandmother, she immediately and without hesitation sat down to make a list of all the things the family should take with them. Horst worried that they didn't have enough suitcases, so he went to see if he could find a couple of cardboard boxes. After he found them, they started filling them and soon realized how poor they really were. The three Sterns hardly had enough clothes to fill two suitcases. They filled the third one with the few pictures and mementoes that had survived. Even after they had finished, none of the suitcases were very heavy.

The month was February and it was quite cold both inside and out, so Horst's family decided they might as well use what little coal and wood they had left to warm in the room and generously fed the pot-bellied stove. The two cardboard boxes went in first followed by the little wood that remained. They ate and retired early for the night.

After breakfast, Erna and Horst decided to take a walk over to the Jewish agency to see how plans for the trip were coming along. When they inquired, the person said, "I am glad that you showed up. We were about to send someone to the place where you live to tell you that all the papers are ready and in order, and that the transport will be ready to leave in a couple of days." He told them to be at the train station's waiting room and someone would give them the new identities, under which they would be traveling. They rushed home to give Selma the good news.

The only thing left to do was for Horst go over to the place where he had been working and tell them what had happened. When he got to the store, Mr. and Mrs. Pancake were happy to see him and to hear of his recent adventure. When he mentioned the organization in Vienna and the opportunity they offered, they looked at each other, and both said that this was definitely something they would look into as well. They told him that in the short time he had been gone, everything had fallen apart. Orders had been cancelled and they could no longer afford to pay for shipments that arrived. There was no other choice but to send them back. He had to let the few people who had worked for him go, and that's when Horst noticed how quiet it was with the machinery at a standstill. Mr. and Mrs. Pancake had thought about leaving but had no idea of how to go about it, so they were really happy to hear the news that Horst had shared with them. Horst hugged them goodbye. He wouldn't see them again for another six years.

After saying goodbye to a few other people he knew, Horst realized that he had spent five miserable years in Hungary but was also thankful they had been allowed to live there. Looking back, he knows that if they hadn't been welcomed, sooner or later, the Nazis would have gotten them and they would have ended up as another statistic.

Days flew by, and by the time it was their last night in Budapest, the Stern family had run out of things to burn for heat. Selma came up with the idea of burning their few pieces of furniture, since they couldn't take any of it with them anyway. Horst took the small axe to their few pieces and they decided to take advantage of the furniture-infused inferno and heat enough water for each of them to take a sponge bath. Enough wood remained for them to get the stove going on their last morning. That was the first time they woke up in a warm room and it was thanks to his grandmother, who was always the first one up in the morning. As they left for the train station that morning, most of their neighbors stood outside and said goodbye to the Stern family.

It was quite a walk to the station, but Selma kept up like the trooper she was.

At the station, they ended up in a big waiting room where there was a large group of people sitting with their suitcases or just standing around. Not long after, a young man came and announced that people going to Vienna needed to step forward, give their names, and receive their train tickets and exit visas.

Shortly after this, everyone got on the train and settled into their seats. It seemed that, like the Sterns, everyone in the compartment was preoccupied with thoughts of getting out of the country and starting new lives elsewhere. The leader spoke up and said, "My name is unimportant; I have done this before, so don't worry."

Each passenger received some papers and was asked to look at them closely. He told them to remember the names that they were given for traveling. If, for some reason, the border guard should ask for identification, they were to hand him the papers. Smiling, he reassured them that all the border guards had been taken care of.

The train pulled out on time and the Sterns were on their way. At the beginning of the journey, no one spoke very much, as everyone was lost in thought of what might happen. But as the train sped up, people relaxed and began to introduce themselves to each other. The Sterns did the same. To their great surprise, they saw Felicia, Uncle Robert's wife, whom they hadn't seen, except for a few times, since she got back from the Bergen-Belsen concentration camp. Robert never made it back. He wound up in Auschwitz, in Poland, and was exterminated just as countless others were.

When Felicia returned from Bergen-Belsen, Erna and Horst had helped her reclaim some of the valuables that she and Robert had buried, for safe keeping, in the cellar of the house where they lived. After that encounter, they never saw her again. So, the surprise was mutual when they saw her sitting there no more than six feet away, in the same row but on the other side of the aisle. What a coincidence that they should all end up on the same transport, on the same day.

Felicia wasn't alone. Despite the proximity of her former in-laws, she was very much engaged with one of the other passengers. Seeing this public display of affection reminded Horst of his Uncle Robert. He thought about the preventable circumstances that led to his uncle's death. The events replayed in his mind.

There was one reason that the Nazis might have targeted Robert for capture if they had seen him. For as far back as Horst could remember, his uncle had to walk with the help of a cane as a result of being plagued by thrombus phlebitis. There was a blood clot in the vein of his right leg. At one point, when it bothered him, his doctor put him into a private clinic for treatments. The doctor, Robert, and Felicia found it best for him to be off the street where his infirmity was visible.

Everything went well in the clinic and the patients weren't bothered by the Nazis. Robert and Felicia stayed there until one of Robert's business associates told them that he could secure them legal papers, proving they were Christian Hungarian citizens. With so many official looking papers, they felt safe enough to leave the clinic and go into hiding.

This friend of Robert and Felicia's also secured a small apartment for them in the Buda section of Budapest and assured them that they would be safe there. The Sterns learned of these circumstances from Felicia when she came back from Bergen-Belsen. She also told them that for this service, their friend charged them quite a bit of money. Robert paid him, in full, in cash. Then she told them that Robert's business associate, and friend, who went through all that trouble to secure them the life-saving papers, was also the person who turned them into the police the next day.

Felicia wanted to confront the man and knew the address of where he lived, she asked Erna and Horst to go along for support. She then decided to find a Russian soldier and tell her story to him in the hope that he would help her gain entry into their apartment. Felicia spoke in perfect Polish because she was born and raised there and she also spoke a little bit of Russian. There were still plenty of Russian soldiers walking on the streets at this time. After about twenty minutes of her talking to several of them, she found one who not only spoke polish, but who also happened to be a Russian Jew. After hearing her story, he told her to lead the way.

They reached the address and knocked on the door. A woman opened it and seeing the Russian soldier, she turned rather pale. Felicia immediately noticed that the woman was wearing her robe. She recognized it as hers because it was monogrammed with F. T. for Felicia Treistman, her maiden name. She asked the woman where her husband was, she told them that toward the end of the war he was inducted by Nylos (The Hungarian Nazi Party) and that she hadn't seen him since. She knew about his activities but couldn't do anything about it. Horst's aunt asked her if she had any objection to their going through her things. She just told them to go ahead.

Horst's aunt recovered most of the wardrobe she had left behind. She even salvaged most of the valuables, among them a dozen expensive Swiss watches, two of which she gave to the soldier for his assistance and, finally, they left. When Horst asked her if he could have one of the watches as a memento of his uncle, she told him, "Maybe, later." Later never arrived.

Apparently, Robert had checked out of the hospital without letting anyone know, and when they was realized that he was gone, it was the responsibility of the clinic staff to contact the police and report that one of their patients was missing. Had they not done this, the whole clinic would have been closed down and all of the patients would be sent to Germany with the next transport when the Nazis conducted one of their routine spot checks again.

As this was going on none of the other Sterns were aware of the situation and one night they were suddenly awakened, at two in the morning, by two men dressed in civilian clothes who told them that they were with the Gestapo. They were told to get dressed because they had something important to discuss with them. The men asked if the family knew Robert Stern and his wife Felicia Stern, maiden name, Treistman. Once they responded that they did, the interview began.

The authorities grilled the family for over two hours. First they asked the family if they knew that Robert Stern was in the hospital and wanted to know when they had last seen him. The Sterns admitted that they visited him in the hospital and mentioned that it seemed that he had been making progress with his recovery. That's when they were told that he had made a miraculous recovery because he had disappeared from the hospital and they wanted to know if the Sterns had any knowledge of where he and his wife might have gone.

The family explained to the men, repeatedly, that Robert and his wife didn't confide in them and that they had no idea of where they could be. Finally, the interrogation ended. As they were leaving, they told the Sterns to each pack a small suitcase and be ready to leave momentarily because if Selma, Erna, and Horst couldn't find them within eight hours, they would be back to take the three of them instead. They were warned to dress warmly.

Horst later wrote, "Thinking about it now, I can only say, that no one has the right to play with the freedom of his family, in exchange for their own. They should have known that there was a price to pay for their actions." Sleep eluded the Sterns for the next couple of nights as they constantly listened for footsteps on the stairwell that might signal their demise. Exhausted and with frayed nerves, it took several days for them to relax. They concluded that because no one had come yet, they must have caught up with Robert and Felicia. After the war, someone informed them that Robert's escape had cost the lives of all the other patients at the clinic and some of the doctors as well. As Horst watched Felicia on the train, he relived all of this in his mind and he pondered that if Robert and Felicia stayed where they were, because the clinic was located in the ghetto, all of the other people in the clinic might have survived just as he, Selma, and Erna did.

The train made good time. There were a few uncertain moments when the train approached the Austrian border at Bamberg. A Russian border guard boarded the train and started walking through, looking left and right and then, without saying a word, disembarked. Everybody sighed with relief when at last, the train began to move once again. They weren't the first people to get out of Hungary this way and they hoped they weren't the last but soon after their trip the Russians closed the border. They were very lucky because after that point, nothing got in or out.

The journey by rail continued until the train stopped at the Wiener Neustadt Railway Station where a truck waited to collect the passengers. After a short drive, they were back at the place where Erna and Horst had begun this adventure but this time they had Selma with them.

16

LIFE IN A DP CAMP

The first leg of a new life began that day in 1945 in Vienna for Horst, 17 years of age, his mother Erna, 51 years of age, and his grandmother Selma, 79 years of age. All three wondered what the future had in store for them. Upon their arrival, they were immediately led to the familiar, large, dining room where they were served a hot meal and told that as soon as they finished eating, they should get ready to be interviewed, just as Erna and Horst had been the last time. After a good meal, they returned to the office and waited for their interviews.

After a short wait, an officer called the three Sterns into another office, which was quite spacious. Erna went first followed by Horst. He answered their questions such as his name, where he was born and he provided a short history of where they had been during the war. Everything was going smoothly, until it was his grandmother's turn to be interviewed. Time seemed to stand still when Selma spoke. Again, her advanced age created quite a stir. The interviewer asked Selma, rather sheepishly, if she could recite a Hebrew prayer. She smiled at him and in a clear voice started to recite a prayer she had learned as a child, *Boruch ato Adonai*, and on she went. Selma's grandson fondly remembers it this way:

"*You could hear a pin drop in the room and see a few tears in people's eyes. Damn, breaks me up writing this. Following her prayer, Selma was asked to sign her name to the document. She did as asked in her beautiful handwriting, and when she had finished signing it, the document went around for everybody to 'ooh and ahh' over. She was an amazing woman."* (Stern, 2006)

Even in his later years, Horst remembered his grandmother's handwriting. Using it, Selma once created a special gift for her grandson. At 85 years old she had penned a handwritten pamphlet, from memory, with poems from some of the best poets Europe had to offer at the time. Although he treasured it for years, he later had the opportunity to gift that pamphlet and other memorabilia to the Berlin Jewish Museum, so he could rest with the knowledge that "others might take a minute to make her acquaintance and meet a great lady." Horst's love for her is evident:

"Many a night, in those past years in Budapest, when life was hard and our stomachs empty, when we went to bed early, just to get warm, I would ask Oma to please recite some of her poems, and when she did, I became a happy little kid, and not much later a happy big kid, and now that writing about it, I am a happy old man, with tears in my eyes. Those poems still ring in my ears. You gathered by now, that I loved this woman." (Stern, 2006)

After the interviews were over, it was time for medical examinations. Following a chest x-ray, Horst was informed that he had a scar on his lung from an earlier injury that fortunately healed on its own, most likely as the result of eating a better diet after the war. The three of them were led to a room, which held cots on which they could sleep.

For the first time in as long as Horst could remember, they received three good meals a day. The Sterns didn't know what to expect but were grateful for anything that came to them. They knew that the place they were in was just a transit stop and as soon as they could put together another group, they would be moving on. Three days later, their names were posted and they were off on the next part of their journey, it was just one of many more to come.

Horst, Selma, and Erna were told that their next stop would be in Bavaria in Germany, a small town by the name of Ainring. It was an unforgettable and beautiful train ride. Horst later commented that real locomotives were used in those days, known as Iron Horses in the United States. The scenery was breathtaking and they gazed at the snowcapped mountains of mid-February in the distance.

A bus awaited the family as they arrived at the station in Ainring and they were immediately transported to the Displaced Persons camp, which became their home for the next three months. The camp turned out to be a collection point for concentration camp survivors from all over Europe. This DP camp was strictly for Jewish survivors, unlike those reserved for European gentiles. There were those that also contained Nazi sympathizers, men who came from the Ukraine, Poland, the Netherlands, Hungary, Rumania, France, and other European countries. When Germany lost the war, they were afraid to go back to where they came from, for fear that they would be hung from the first light pole upon their return.

Ainring was once occupied by the German Luftwaffe (the German Air Force). The three Sterns were given one of the rooms, in a barrack, that consisting of army cots, a small table, a few chairs, and a shelf for incidentals. The room even had curtains on the windows, and the part Horst loved the most, they had real bathrooms at the end of the hall (on the same floor) with showers, hot running water, and toilets. Hot water radiators heated the rooms and as far as the Sterns were concerned it might as well have been The Ritz. Another barrack served as an army style mess hall that served three meals a day.

In addition to comfortable accommodations and good food, there was a community hall where movies were shown three times a week and dances held on weekends. Also, they each began to receive a weekly care package. The first one they received came as a shock to them. It contained chocolate, a can of Nestle milk, a can of Spam, and other things. To top it off, there was a whole carton of cigarettes. The brand were new to them, as those were the first American cigarettes that they had ever seen, brands such as

Chesterfield, Lucky Strikes, Phillip Morris, and Camels. He didn't smoke in those days, though.

There was an even bigger surprise in store for Horst and his family as they were directed to another barrack down the street. Once there, it was as if they had entered a department store. The room before them was full of men's and women's clothing, in all sizes. Everything was available from shoes to underwear. Someone working there told them they could select two outfits each and helped them find the right sizes.

Their own clothes had been the cheapest available at the time and were purchased, secondhand, at the flea market in Budapest. The lady who helped them select their new outfits explained that all the items there were donations from people living in the United States and Horst and his family couldn't have been more grateful.

While Horst didn't smoke and had no need for the care package cigarettes, Erna was in seventh heaven. Back in the Ghetto, she would exchange her portion of bread for some tobacco. He never let on that he knew about her exchanges and it was hard for him to understand her addiction at the time. Unfortunately, it didn't take him long to find out for himself.

When he was still 17 years old, it seemed to him that everybody in the camp was smoking except him, so one day he lit up a Lucky Strike to give it a try. He says,

"*All I got out of it was that I became woozy in the head and instead of quitting right then and there, I had to prove to myself that real men don't quit... It didn't take me long before I was hooked.*" (Stern, 2006)

He was only able to kick his habit 30 years later and with the help of a hypnotist.

Whether the family received any spending money or not, Horst didn't know but felt that they most likely received some because they were charged one German Mark entrance fee to get into the movie house, which was the equivalent to about 25 cents and it was prohibited to sell anything they received in the camp. Their spending money had to come from somewhere.

Selling may not have been permitted, but the black market was in full swing, and the authorities just looked the other way. Cigarettes, chocolate, Nylon stockings, and of course, canned goods were the unofficial currencies of the camp. Anytime they needed some money, they sold some cigarettes, which gave them enough spending money for incidentals, mostly for movie tickets. All other necessities, like toothbrushes and soap, were regularly provided for them.

On a few occasions the three Sterns took an excursion trip to Berchtesgaden. It was a fairly short trip by steam locomotive but what a ride it was! It was such a beautiful town. Horst felt that it was no wonder that Adolf Hitler had his hideaway, The Eagle's Nest, there.

After settling into their new environment, Horst and his family began to notice that there was tension among the people in the camp.

"You would think that people who had suffered for so long, spent years in concentration camps just for being born into the Jewish faith, and after six million of them were exterminated by the Hitler regime, they would, or could, get along amongst themselves. You would be wrong." (Stern, 2006)

Horst found it appalling to see grown men at each other's throats for minor reasons when once they had shared a plank as a bed in a concentration camp. Yet, considering the circumstances, perhaps such squabbles should have been expected. In the DP camps, people who had survived the war were thrown together. Here, strangers who had nothing more in common than sharing a common faith, struggles, and loss, suddenly had to coexist in close proximity to one another. The similarity ended with their wartime experiences, which meant they wouldn't always see eye to eye.

Horst felt that some of these disagreements stemmed from the premise that individuals from every nationality or religion thought that they were the chosen people. In an effort to prove this, they have tried to destroy one another, and have done so since the beginning of time. In the DP camp, they proved themselves by beating each other up. These conflicts mainly occurred between people from different countries. People from one country felt those from other countries were inferior.

Residents of the DP camp shared a common language, Yiddish (a blend of German dialect with words from Hebrew with elements of Russian, Polish, and other eastern European languages), but resented the differing accents with which it was spoken. It really surprised Horst that there they were, living in a DP camp, with other people of the Jewish faith, survivors from the death camps, Poland, Hungary, Romania and various other places, and they were at each other's throats over ethnicity. The situation escalated when the name-calling began with insults such as, "You dirty Polack," or "You dirty Hungarian Gypsy." He has continued to witness this phenomenon of human behavior over and over again in his many years since.

"What will it take for mankind to realize that once one is put onto this earth one has only a short time to make it a better place to live on and that time has the nasty habit of slipping through one's fingers with such speed that most of us forget to enjoy the time we do have? In other words, from the time one is born to the time one dies is only a short time and there are better things to advocate than hate. It will never cease to amaze me how so-called intelligent people can, and will, commit murder in the name of their God and feel no remorse whatsoever for what they have done." (Stern, 2006)

17

WAITING FOR IMMIGRATION

A day came when the Stern family was called into the office and they were asked if they had any preference as to where they would like to immigrate. When they expressed that the United States would be their first choice, they were told that the people in charge would get back to them about it. Within a week they were called back into the office and were told by the person who handled their case that because they were born in Berlin, and had lived there for a considerable amount of time, it would be to their advantage to go back there and put in a petition for immigration in Berlin. If they agreed to that, he would make the necessary arrangements to get them there.

Three weeks passed before the Sterns were notified to go to the office at Ainring, where they received good news. Everything had been arranged and in a couple of days they would be on their way to Berlin. Their first stop would be Munich, where they would have to spend a few days and from there they would travel nonstop to Berlin. Upon their arrival, there was someone holding up a sign for them to follow.

As they disembarked at their first stop, the family was stunned by the complete devastation before them. Horst observed that the American Air Force had done a thorough job. They missed a house here and there but all in all, if he were to rate them on a scale of one through ten, he would give them a nine and a half because of the few houses still standing. After a bus ride, of about 30 minutes, they arrived at a big campsite on the outskirts of Munich where they were told to find their belongings. It almost became routine; small room, army cots for the three of them, and after their traveling papers were looked at, they were told not to get too comfortable because they wouldn't be there long enough to call this home. And that was it.

As they arrived in Berlin, they were once again picked up and taken straight to the Schlachtensee DP Camp, which was about a 30-minute ride by subway to the center of the city. Berlin in 1946 was in a shambles but Horst felt little distress over it because there were so many bad memories for him there. He explains it with little emotion in his book:

"I lived there for the first 12 years of my life, and all I can remember is fear, confusion, and my escape into exile, involuntarily, in order not to be put down like a rabid dog. Well, I survived. It was a pleasure to see Berlin in 1946 with all its glory bombed into submission." (Stern, 2006)

Before them, they saw complete devastation that included blocks without a home left standing but there were survivors determined to keep going. They would eventually clean up and rebuild the city of Berlin.

Once they arrived at the camp, they were directed to their new living quarters. The room was a replica of the room they had left the night before, the same identical army cots and everything else. They were housed far enough from the city that there was very little damage there. The nearest suburb, Zehlendorf, was three elevated train stops away from their new DP camp and Horst really got to know it quite well in the time he lived there.

The newest camp was huge, actually housing up to 5,000 Jewish refugees mostly from Eastern Europe who were awaiting departure for the USA and Palestine. As a result of its vast size, it took the family longer to get familiar with this camp. It took about a week to get to know where all the offices were located, which they would need to visit frequently. It was made up of German Army barracks and one of them became home to Horst, Erna, and Selma for almost two long, eventful, years. Here they dreamed of better lives, had promises made and had promises broken. Once again, there were many people housed together in a mixture of nationalities but Horst remained detached from all that.

DP Camp Arrivals. Photo: Public Domain

Considering what the Sterns had gone through since they had left their room in Hungary, the train rides, bus rides, and stays in four camps in as little as three months, everything went remarkably smoothly or at least as much as could be expected. Through it all, Horst's grandmother always had a smile on her face and never complained about anything. As far as she was concerned as long as they were together, she was happy.

This United Nations Relief and Rehabilitation Administration (UNRRA) camp was run by an American officer and six other uniformed officers. There were no restrictions on coming or going. Each DP resident was given a slip of paper stating that they were residents of the camp and under the protection of the USA Government.

Horst soon met some other survivors who were around his age. Most of them were products of mixed marriages where either the father or the mother was Jewish and the other a gentile. According to Horst, 98 percent of them had lost at least one parent to the death camps. Most only had one parent who had survived the Holocaust. Two of them became very close friends of Horst's. One was Bernhard Wiesengrund who was a survivor of Bergen-Belsen. The other was Alexander Pasternack who came from Poland and had survived one of the camps there.

Alexander, known to his friends as Ali, told Horst that when the Germans invaded Poland in 1939, he was living in Berlin with his parents. His mother was a German gentile who had married a Polish Jew. When the Germans repatriated all Polish Jews, his parents went with him to Poland. While shopping one day in Warsaw, Ali and his parents were all picked up by the police. He and his father ended up in one camp, and his mother in another. Ali and his father survived and ended up in Berlin and his father began the search for his wife through the Red Cross, but to no avail. Eventually, he met a woman, remarried, and had another child.

Ali decided to get out of Germany and ended up in the DP camp in Schlachtensee. He went to Israel in 1948 and served in the Israeli Army where he worked up as an airplane mechanic. In the 1950s, Horst received a letter from Ali saying that he had been contacted by an agency that specialized in finding concentration camp survivors and trying to reunite them with lost family members. The letter told him that his mother was alive and well and had never given up searching for him and after all those years she had finally found him. She was living in Paris. Ali went over there to reunite with her. For years, Horst hoped that Alexander Pasternak might still be alive and that he might be able to resume contact with him.

Perhaps it was unlikely that Ali and Horst might find each other after so many years but there was precedence for this unlikely hope. He shared the following story:

"I was nine years old and had a friend who was a year younger, Heinz Perlhefter. His father was Hungarian, and mother born in Germany, both of them of the Jewish faith. We lived in the same apartment house in Berlin and we used to play together. One day they were suddenly gone. At the time I never even gave it a second thought, so many things happened in such a short time.

Then, one day, Erna and I were walking down Kiraly Utca [Street] in Budapest in 1942, and what a surprise to see Heinz and his parents doing the same thing. We renewed our friendship, got together a few times until his father was picked up by the Nazis, right off the street, and the last thing his wife heard about him was that he ended up in one of those slave-labor battalions in Russia, from where he never made it back.

We went our separate ways again, and wouldn't you know? Erna and I were walking down a street in Haifa, Israel, and whom do we run into? You guessed it, my friend Heinz with his mother. This was in 1950. They both had joined a Kibbutz and lived there happily." (Stern, 2006)

Unfortunately, Horst lost contact with them shortly thereafter. He says now that, "It's a big planet, but a small world."

When the Stern family finally got to Berlin, they were informed about the laws pertaining to immigration to the United States, such as facts about eligibility. Those who could prove that they were residing in the American, British, French Zones or sectors in Germany, in or before a certain date in February of 1946, were eligible to immigrate to the United States without the need of a sponsor.

Of all the young people Horst knew, there was only one who qualified. His name was Kurt Sorge. He admits though that the reason he remembers it so well is because the two of them spent ten days in jail together, in the Russian sector of Berlin when they were accused of being spies for the Americans. While in jail, Kurt discussed his pending departure to the USA.

The rest of the group had to wait for their quota, which was based on place of birth. He realized that if he had been born in Switzerland, Canada, or maybe even in Australia, he wouldn't have to wait very long, he was told that their quota was never filled.

If a displaced person had a relative living in the States, they also had a chance at immigration, provided the relative was willing and able to sponsor the displaced person. The sponsors would have to take responsibility for whatever the immigrant did for the next five years, which was when one could apply for citizenship. It wasn't common for someone to come up with a sponsor. Personally, he never knew of anyone who did that.

Every three or four months a new rumor would go around that the date had been extended and that those who could prove that they had resided in the aforementioned zones would be eligible for a visa to immigrate to the United States. No one really knew who started the rumors, but they worked as intended. It gave them hope, at least temporarily.

The three Sterns had settled nicely into their one-room home. Actually, they had been living that way for so many years that if Horst had his own room he doubted he would've been comfortable in it all alone. Meanwhile, he had turned 18 and this was the first time in a long

time that he didn't have to worry about anything. The family had free room and board, free hospitalization and they didn't have to pay any taxes. It was far from perfect, though. The trouble with living like that was that they all had too much time on their hands, so they tried to do something about it.

Erna applied for a job at the camp kitchen and started working there the next day. Not long after, the cook who had been in charge got his papers for immigration to the States. His leaving left Erna temporarily in charge of the kitchen or at least until they could find another cook to replace him. It appeared that she did a good job because they never replaced the cook and the job was hers.

According to Horst, his mother was never one to sit on her hands or complain that she couldn't handle a task. In the case of the camp kitchen position, she did such a good job that the person in charge of the kitchen asked her if she would be interested in specializing in dietary cooking. Erna agreed to take some classes and was soon certified.

In lieu of pay, Erna received additional care packages, each containing more cartons of cigarettes and all kinds of canned goods. Erna sent most of the contents to her sister Rosa and Rosa's husband. They had survived the war and the bombings in Berlin, but it hadn't been easy.

Theirs was a mixed marriage. Rosa was a Jew and her husband, a gentile. Not only were they ostracized and treated harshly but they received fewer food stamps than the rest of the population and they weren't welcomed anywhere. They clearly stood out because she had to wear the Star of David so they decided it would be better if he went out by himself.

Horst gave his uncle credit for standing by his aunt for so many years. The food packages Erna supplied them with made life a bit easier for them, especially the cartons of cigarettes, which were more valuable than money.

Sometimes it appears that today's generation has forgotten how difficult times were for the general German population in 1946. So much of the city was destroyed. It took time for stores to reopen, food was extremely scarce and the citizens could often be seen at the gates of the camp in the hopes of bartering valuables for food or cigarettes. Horst recalled the scene with his characteristically direct candor:

"It was kind of pleasurable, but also pathetic to see those Germans come to the gate of the camp, bartering all kinds of valuables, from wedding rings, diamonds, fur coats, anything that had of any value for food or even cigarettes. The black-market was booming, and most of these people were victims of the times, but it was impossible for me to erase the picture of them standing not that long ago on the streets of Berlin screeching their adoration to that butcher of humanity." (Stern, 2006)

Over the years, Horst became more at ease with his feelings about Germany and the past but he admits that when he encounters a German in his age group or older, his defense mechanism "rings a little bell within", and he immediately wonders where the person was during the war.

During the two years he lived in Ainring, Horst came across quite a few Germans. He often came right out and asked if they were aware of all the concentration camps and the treatment of the Jews in Berlin. None would admit that they knew of any of wrong doing towards them. Some even told him that they knew some Jewish people, but that they had moved away.

Horst, Bernhard, and Ali were getting bored with nothing to do but wait for evening to arrive so they could go to the nearest town and either dance, drink, or meet some ladies. The only jobs that were available in camp were either working in the motor pool, or joining the camp police force, which consisted of volunteer residents. Each volunteer received a baton, stood at the gate and monitored the comings and goings of all who entered the facilities as well as checking that anyone coming in had the right identification to enter the camp. Horst thought the day shift looked all right, but the night shift wasn't much to look forward to.

The camp had quite a large motor pool and they were always looking for people to work there. The three young men talked it over and came to the conclusion that they might have an opportunity to learn something, including how to drive a car, and eventually they all did. None of them had the opportunity during the war to learn a trade, with the exception of slave labor, which included skills like the of digging tank traps and holes for the dead (and almost dead). All three applied and were hired for the motor pool.

The motor pool consisted mainly of army vehicles, Jeeps, weapons carriers, ambulances, a six by six, 2.5 ton truck, and one or two German cars for the "hotshots" in camp. Their boss was a former German Army mechanic, and Horst learned quickly that when he said to clean the vehicle from top to bottom, he meant it. He even went so far as to check their work with the white glove test.

As the driver maneuvered the Jeep over the pit so Horst could clean the vehicle from underneath, the young man watched every move. One day, he asked the man in charge of this operation what it would take to learn to operate and drive one of the cars. The man looked at Horst and asked him if he had a cigarette. He gave him a pack and told him to keep the whole thing. That was the beginning of Horst's driving journey.

The driver explained what each pedal's function was and the fundamentals of what it took to put a jeep into motion. Before long, Horst took the first step. After cleaning the engine, he looked around for the fellow who drove the car, but there was no sight of him so he decided to take the opportunity to do it himself. He learned quickly that it wasn't as easy as it looked, he stalled the engine three times in as many minutes by letting the clutch out too fast. The mechanic in charge was watching Horst, but instead of yelling or losing his temper, he called all of the workers together and told them that he would teach them the fundamentals of operating a motor vehicle. Then he asked for cigarettes and that's when they realized that not all Germans were bad.

They had seen so much evil perpetrated by the Germans for so many years that they were touched by this little gesture of goodwill (for a price). True to his word, every day he took some time to first explain what makes an engine run and after that he took one of the jeeps and drove with each one of them around the motor pool.

After about a week, he felt it would be all right for the workers to handle driving on their own but he told them that if they were serious about getting a driver's license, they would have to go to a driving school and take a test. Later, Horst did just that and he still has that license today. Although, he has no plans to go to Germany to use it again. Either way, he feels that the cigarettes were well-spent.

The seven young men who worked in the motor pool looked forward to going out at night. After they finished work each day, they went home, showered, ate something, and went off to find fun. They were making up for lost time, years when they could do little else but fight for survival. The men, including Horst, found places in Berlin that fulfilled all of their needs, the details of which will be omitted here and left to the imagination of the reader but if you were to ask him directly, he would give you an earful. To get there, they had to take the Stadt-Bahn, which is like the subway train except that it was actually an elevated train that connected all of Berlin.

The group had discovered a place in Zehlendorf, about three stops away on the elevated route. It was a coffee shop, but when the door was opened, one could see that it had a dance floor and on weekends there was live music. There was a four-piece orchestra that consisted of a violin player, a trumpet player, an accordion player, and a drummer. They played mainly American dance music and a few old German tunes. To the young men, they sounded great, but they admittedly had little to compare it to because they had been out of action for so long.

Naturally, the coffee house served coffee, but also cakes, Coca-Cola, beer, and wine by the glass or bottle but if liquor was preferred the patrons had to supply their own. The first time Horst and the others went there they all paid in cash but soon discovered that cigarettes or any kind of canned food was preferred. Two packs of Camels bought them a bottle of wine. Beer was much cheaper.

Horst was surprised at how many young women went to these places just to have some fun. When it came to dancing, he had no experience but the girls showed him how to dance and helped him gain experience in other areas as well. These wild weekends went on for quite a while until one day, the roof fell in.

Rumors circulated that the American consul had changed the date for immigrating but by this time no one paid them any attention. One day the subject came up and Horst and his friends began to talk about what they would do if they ever got out of Germany. They decided they wanted to go to any other country and figured that anything would be better than remaining in Germany.

That's when Horst's grandmother surprised him and Erna by announcing that she had made up her mind to stay in Germany and spend the few years she had left to live with her other daughter in Berlin. This way she didn't have to learn a new language in order to communicate with the rest of the population. At 80 years old, she felt she was getting too old to become a world traveler.

Horst and his mother tried to talk Selma out of her decision but she wouldn't hear it, so they packed her few belongings and with very mixed emotions, escorted her over to where she would live from then on. When they returned to their room in camp that night it just didn't feel right. Erna and Horst felt guilty but after talking it over they realized that although this wasn't what they wanted, it was Selma's choice and they had to respect it.

While straightening out the room, Erna noticed that her mother had left some of the knitting she had been working on. They decided to take it with them the next time they visited he, but before they had the chance to do that, they received a letter from Selma saying that everything was just fine but she wished that she had finished her knitting in camp. Horst and Erna saw this as a red flag, a call for help, and immediately went to Selma the next day.

As they walked into the apartment, they were shocked to see that his uncle had transformed the whole apartment into a safety zone. He had wrapped all the chair legs with some old rags, including the legs of the piano. All of this was to make sure that Horst's grandmother couldn't bang against them with her shoe or leave a scratch on the wood. They knew that his uncle was a little odd but this was crazy behavior, even for him. To top this, she wasn't allowed in the kitchen to cook or even to heat up some water for tea fearing that she might drop something and ruin the linoleum flooring.

They didn't say anything, for Horst's aunt's sake, but years later she confided in them that he wasn't an easy man to live with, but she stayed with him because he had stayed with her when it counted the most. He never laid a hand on her but she took his verbal abuse for years.

Horst and Erna told his aunt and uncle that this arrangement wasn't working out and that Selma would be better off with them and that was the way they left it. Selma's dream of living out the remainder of her life peacefully came to a sudden end. During the ordeal she didn't say a word but when they were back in camp, in their little room, her eyes lit up and all she said was, "Home!"

Both Horst and his mother had really missed Selma during the short time that she was gone and it made her happy to hear it. That night, Horst stayed home for a change and they celebrated his grandmother's return. Meanwhile, Selma finally confided in them that she didn't really want to go and live with her other daughter and her husband but she thought it would make it easier for them. She felt it would give them a better chance of immigrating, she knew that the chances for a person of her age going were slim to none.

The three Sterns settled back into a routine of working, listening to all the rumors and continuing to hope that all the waiting would soon come to an end. Meanwhile, Horst graduated and received his driver's license in camp and subsequently got promoted to chauffeur. He drove UNRRA personnel around Berlin.

"This lasted for a few months, and being 19 years old with a mentality of a 13 year old, I drove those cars like a cowboy out on the range. It didn't take long before enough complaints about my driving accumulated with the expected result that I was fired before I had the chance to kill someone, including myself." (Stern, 2006)

Now, he wonders how he lasted as long as he did. He says he would have fired himself long before. He wasn't too bothered by unemployment. He knew there was always a shortage of camp police and they were always hiring young men. The older residents were too busy making good money on the black market.

As far as Horst was concerned, he had enough money in all of those cartons of cigarettes he received from his weekly care packages, plus the cartons he received for working in the camp. Admittedly, all he was interested in was having a good time, getting drunk on booze and getting the ladies but just like the other men he loved them and left them. They never got serious with any of the German *Fraülein*.

18

EVERYONE LOVES A MAN IN UNIFORM

Horst put in his application for the police job and got accepted. Naturally, as the youngest member, he got the graveyard shift but it was surprisingly easier than he thought it would be. There were always two on duty at the gate and nothing much happened at night. They switched every two hours. He would "curl up and take a snooze," and then the other guy would do the same. Before they knew it, it was morning again. Three eight-hour shifts, rotating every other week kept him out of trouble, for a while at least.

Horst appreciated that uniforms were supplied by the camps for this position. They were American uniforms that had been dyed black and, according to him, were rather sharp-looking with an International Rescue Organization (IRO is the organization that replaced the UNNRA) emblem stenciled on the sleeve of the shirt and jacket. A cap was also included, which was worn at a tilt. Most especially, Horst appreciated the effect that the uniforms had on the girls. Some things never change and he points out that women lose their minds when it comes to men in uniforms.

But the uniform was almost his undoing. It started quite innocently. Their DP camp was in the American sector and the Russian zone was less than two miles from it. At the end of the war, Germany was divided amongst the Allies at the time. Part went to

France, another part became the English zone, another part went to the Russians, and part became the American zone. Berlin, the former capital city of Germany, was divided amongst the four powers, into sectors. There was no border between the American and Russian zones and anyone could pass back and forth without difficulty. Horst had been into the Russian zone of Berlin quite a few times over the course of three weeks because he had a formed a relationship with a beautiful fräulein, who he met in one the hangouts he used to frequent. After a night out on the town he took her home to her place as he had done previously and stayed the night.

Late into the evening there was a loud knock on the front door, which they tried to ignore. All of a sudden, the door flew off its hinges and three Vopos, the East Berlin police force, burst in, yelling. They were warned not to move and to hold their hands up. They shone a strong beam from a flashlight on the unsuspecting couple. The police instructed Horst to get out of bed nice and slowly, and instructed the Fräulein to stay where she was. It was the stuff that nightmares were made of.

Horst was told to get dressed and when he finished he was handcuffed and escorted down the stairs. Before he could comprehend what was really happening, he was sitting in a speeding car, siren blaring. After the car stopped, he was taken out and escorted into a building. Someone removed his handcuffs and he was immediately fingerprinted, photographed, and marched down a corridor and forced into a cell.

The cell door slammed shut and Horst looked around. A small light bulb threw off enough light to make out an iron cot against the wall with what appeared to be a thin mattress, and that was it. He hadn't had any sleep before he was taken but when he tried to lie down, the cell door opened again and before he knew it, two guards entered and escorted him to an office. Behind the desk sat a uniformed officer of the Russian army, his chest covered with all kinds of medals. Next to him sat a big German shepherd that was glaring at Horst and another person in civilian clothing who turned out to be an interpreter. That is when the nightmare began.

The barrage of questions began with them asking his name. Then he was asked, "Where do you live and what are you doing in the Russian zone in the middle of the night?" The group then wanted to know what kind of uniform he was wearing, where he was born, and the names of his parents. He said the last question "tickled" him because he was so tired, so he claimed he had no father and that his mother was special. The officer looked at him and let this answer slide but then wanted Horst to tell his story. He started telling the story of his girlfriend when he was interrupted by the officer's loud voice demanding, "Who sent you?" and continued drilling him with other questions. "What is the reason for you being here in the Russian zone? Who is this girl you are talking about? Where does she work? How long and how many times have you been to the Russian Zone? What has that girl been telling you?"

He never had a chance to answer any of the questions and doubts that the officer expected an answer to any of them. So, when the questioning finally ended, the officer looked at Horst waited, which he took as a sign to answer some of the questions. He began:

"My name is Horst Stern, born here in Berlin in 1928. To the question of what I was doing here in the Russian zone? I was trying to make love to my girlfriend when I was interrupted right in the middle of it. I have known her for about three weeks, and since she happens to live here in the Russian zone, we have spent our nights at her place.

Next I am asked, what kind of uniform is that I am wearing? It originally belonged to the American army, and was dyed black, and given to the O.R.T, which gave them to the camp police of which I am a member, and I am to wear while I am either on or off the job." (Stern, 2006)

When he asked where the camp was that he was talking about, Horst just stared at him and told him it was about a five-minute car ride from the camp to the Russian zone. After that, he wanted to know if Horst knew the name of the person who was in charge of that camp and if he was wearing an American uniform? He also wanted to know if there were any others in uniform, how many, and their ranks.

Horst was only able to come up with the name of the camp director but he felt that everyone knew his name. Some of the questions made no sense to him and others were asked repeatedly, such as "Who sent you? What were you looking for?" and "Why were you in the Russian sector in the middle of the night?"

After hours of this Horst was told to think about the situation he was in, the officer then said that he hoped that the next time they had a talk, Horst would have something to tell him. With that, he turned around and called the guards to escort him back to the cell. Upon his return to the cell, he discovered that a blanket had appeared and he fell into instant slumber as soon as he hit the cot. It seemed he had just fallen asleep when he was shaken awake by the guard and told to get up because they were going to see the nice man in the office again, he had a few more questions to ask him. Horst was escorted to the same room but the Russian officer wasn't the same one he had seen previously. The dog was also missing but one thing remained the same, a repetition of the same questions.

"Who sent you?"

"Who runs the camp?"

"Where do you live?"

"What did they tell you to look for?"

"What is the purpose of your being here?"

Every time Horst tried to answer one question, the officer went on to the next one. He never really had a chance to answer any one of them so he just kept his mouth shut and let the officer continue. After a while, he looked at Horst and said that if he ever wanted to see his mother again, he better start answering the questions. With that, he called in the guards and told them to take him away.

They escorted him back to his cell where he tried very hard to go to sleep. He recalls that he was getting physically tired and if he had known what it was that they wanted to hear, he might have been able to make something up. Luckily for him, there was nothing he could tell them. It was the same questions over and over then back to the cell for two hours, for the rest of the day. This continued for the next few days. In the few hours he was able to sleep, he could still hear them asking, "Who sent you?"

Horst lost track of how many days had gone by but one morning when the guard came for him, they took a different turn and that's when he noticed that they were on a side street where a black car was waiting for them. He was told to get into the back of the car. Its windows were painted black so he had no way of knowing where they were going.

This time Horst wasn't handcuffed; he thought perhaps they had decided that he wasn't a dangerous criminal after all. It took quite a while before they reached their destination and he had no idea where they were. The car door eventually opened and they were in front of a police station where he was escorted into another cell, larger than the one he had been in before. There was room for four prisoners but there was just one other now and he looked familiar. It turned out to be his friend from camp, Kurt. Shocked to see each other, they shared their stories of what brought them to their current situation. Their stories mirrored each other, only the girls' names and addresses differed.

The two men were dressed identically because Kurt also worked for the camp police. The whole situation was the result of having girlfriends who lived in the wrong location in Berlin.

The interrogations went on and on. Kurt was questioned for two hours straight and after they finished with him, it was Horst's turn. The questions never changed. This went on for days on end.

After three days at this place, they were moved once again. They were transported to a different location, only this time in the middle of the night. The driver spoke and told them that we were about 100 kilometers away from Berlin.

When they finally arrived at their destination, they ended up in a small cell and were told that this time they would be interviewed by higher-ups. They were both dead tired and fell asleep instantly. Early the next morning, the whole process began all over again, two hours of questioning and two hours off. The same questions were asked and the same answers were given.

Eight days had passed since the two young men had been taken and they still had no idea where they were. On the ninth day, Kurt told Horst that he told the interpreter that his immigration papers to the United States would be arriving any day now and that this was his only chance for a better life. The interrogator told him not to worry because where they were being sent they wouldn't need any papers, unless one of them chose to confess and tell them who had sent them there and for what purpose. Day number ten came along and Kurt was interrogated first. This time it seemed to Horst that he was there longer than the previous day and when he finally returned, he just smiled and told Horst that whatever they asked him to do, he should agree to it. He asked him what it was that he would be agreeing to do but Kurt simply told him, "You will see shortly."

Back in the room, Horst was told that if he wanted to get out of there all he had to do was cooperate with them. He didn't even get a chance to say a word when he was told that all he had to do was collect data of who worked at the camp, once he returned there. They requested the ranks and documented evidence of the comings and goings of any ranked, uniformed officers, even if it felt insignificant.

If Horst agreed to all this, not only would they allow him to return but they would also make it worth his while. He was told that Kurt had agreed to the deal and that they would work together on this project. Only one of them had to come back with the data they collected. They would be contacted with the days and times to meet. He was warned that if either of them tried to renege on the deal, they would be found and dealt with accordingly. With that, Horst was escorted back to the cell. He and Kurt didn't say anything, they just looked at each other and after they were fed, they went to sleep. This was the first time that they weren't disturbed and slept right through until morning.

Apprehension set in, the two men had no idea if the Russians could be trusted but true to their word a guard came to the cell door and told them that they were free to go. When they got out on the street a big surprise awaited them. They thought they would have a hard time getting home because they had assumed that they were at least 100 kilometers from home. They soon learned that it had all been a game to their captors. Because of the moving to various locations over the last ten days, they had no way of knowing that rather than being deep within the Russian zone, they were only about a few kilometers from the American sector. They ran and didn't stop until they reached the gate of the camp.

The Vopos didn't return their camp identifications but Horst and Kurt had no problem at the gate. The other residents wanted to know where the two had been for so long. The rumor was that they were abducted by the Russians, which wasn't too far-fetched since it happened not long before. The difference was that those victims had been Jewish and deserted the Russian Army and were looking for asylum at the DP camp. Some of them made it but a few unlucky ones got snatched right off the street, in broad daylight, never to be seen again. He calls them more casualties of the war but explains that was what life like in 1946 and 1947. Horst and Kurt were taken in the beginning of 1948, though. To the rest of the world, they just disappeared into thin air.

When Horst entered their family's room, the first thing Erna did was slap his face and yell at him, "Where the hell have you been for the last ten days?" Then she hugged and kissed the spot on his face that she had just slapped. Selma just looked at him with a big sigh of relief and smiled because he was home, at last, safe and sound.

Horst realized that it was time to report to the camp director's office, where he found Kurt, he was about to disclose everything that had happened to them, in detail, during their absence which included how they were able to make a deal with the Russians in exchange for their release. The director called in an American intelligence officer and asked the two to repeat the entire story to him. After finishing, he was asked to leave the room and wait in the room next door.

After about 20 minutes, he was called back into the room and noticed that Kurt was no longer there. It was Horst's turn to recall everything that happened in the last ten days.

After he finished, Kurt came back into the room and that's when the intelligence officer in charge made them an offer that was easy to refuse.

Upon hearing what the Russians wanted the young men to do,

the American intelligence officer suggested that they return to the Russian zone as soon as they were contacted by the Russian officer. The information the Russians needed would be provided by the camp's intelligence officer. They said that Horst and Kurt would be well-protected during the operation. They both declined the offer, realizing that one wrong move could send them right back to jail and perhaps a one-way ticket to Siberia. The officer understood the reason for their reluctance but cautioned them to restrict their movements and be careful when out at night. For the next month, Horst didn't leave the camp grounds, to the delight of his mother and grandmother.

19

ISRAEL

Kurt, Horst's partner in crime, received his visa to the USA and not long after receiving it, he left. Horst never heard how he made out. He began to organize his thoughts, and all he could think of was, *here we were, the three of us in one room, with no financial worries, everything is paid for like our food, our room, no electric bills, so how come, I am not content?* Perhaps it had something to do with the rumors they had lived with for two years, that one of these days they would get out of there so they could try to make a new life for themselves in a country of their choice. The wait seemed endless and still nothing changed.

Meanwhile, life continued. Horst turned 20 and had no desire to go back to school, even if there was one. He still stuttered, maybe a little less than before but enough to make him self-conscious about it. He didn't know a trade in which he could make a living other than his ditch-digging skills which he learned under duress during his time as a slave laborer. He could drive a car but as he describes "hazardously." He pondered:

"In order to make a living at anything, you first have to have a home in a country were at least you have the chance to make it on your own. Whatever you do accomplish, have the assurance that you can keep that what you have worked so hard for. And the only country I knew of that *had a system like that was the US of A. So far we had wasted over two years, living on rumors and empty promises, or waiting for a miracle to happen."* (Stern, 2006)

It was the middle of April and the War of Independence in Israel had started. With most men Horst's age simply drifting along, waiting for the chance to immigrate anywhere, he thought that if the French Foreign Legion had set up a recruiting station in the camp, they would have hit the jackpot. They were ready to go anywhere, immediately! That's when the Haganah set up a recruiting station right in the middle of the camp. They were looking for volunteers to fight for the independence of Israel, or as Horst says, "to go to Israel and get their asses shot off." The timing couldn't have been more perfect. Psychologically, this was just the thing they needed. It was their ticket out.

Horst admits he was young and foolish. He had also spent half his life in uncertainly and with when this adventure stared him in the face, he couldn't resist the call to go. He wasn't alone. In one day, the camp lost 90 percent of its young people, including the single women.

The hardest part for Horst was trying to justify his decision to his mother and grandmother. He started by explaining that this was his one and only chance to get out of Germany and once the war was over he would assess the situation and see if he could start a productive life for the three of them in Israel, they could follow him there at a later date. He explained that while he was gone, Erna could contact her cousin in New York to see if there was anything she could do to help.

When Horst made the decision to volunteer for the Haganah and go to Israel, he never thought of the consequences of this decision. Some of the volunteers loved it there, served their time and moved on. While some others settled in a *Kibbutz* (a settlement, usually a farm). He is convinced that only the few Zionists who were amongst them knew what was in store for them but Horst and the rest just went to get out of the monotony they were living in.

It took them about a month to put the transport together and when the day finally arrived for Horst to say good bye to his mother and grandmother the consequence of his decision hit him like a ton of bricks. Of course, by that time it was too late so he tried to convince himself that he had done the right thing. He also convinced himself that Erna's cousin would come through with a visa for her and Selma. With him gone, their chances might be better of getting the visas because there would be one less person to vouch for. This realization helped Horst feel better about his decision. He realizes now, that back then, he was an immature 20 year old.

Suddenly, he realized that this would be the first time in his life that he would truly be on his own and wouldn't have to look after anyone but himself. For once, he was free as a bird. There were very few in his transport that had any family left. They were the sole survivors of an extended family and couldn't understand why and how he could leave his mother and grandmother behind. As difficult as it was for him to leave them, he didn't regret it. Although the next three years of his life "were hell," at least it was a hell of his own making and experiencing it made his life far richer.

The transport of volunteers, about 60 strong, including a dozen girls, was put aboard a cargo plane and together they took off toward an unknown fate. It was the first plane ride for all of them and they found it to be relatively enjoyable. After landing in Munich, they spent the night in a DP camp. The next morning, they were put onto two, six-by-six trucks, and again they were on their way. Their moods were light and it didn't take long before someone started to sing and the rest joined in. Most of the songs they sang were German songs with a few Jewish songs mixed in. Their favorite was "Don't Fence Me In."

They traveled through the Black Forest, a trip that left Horst awestruck by its beauty. Eventually, they got to the French border, where they finally stopped at a train station in Lyon. There, they boarded a train that took them to a small village which he later learned was about 40 kilometers from Marseilles. Another truck ride followed to take them to their final destination in Europe before they boarded the ship to Israel.

Little more than a clearing in a forest, this accommodation

wasn't just another camp, but more of a tent city. It was set up with the permission of the French government to be used temporarily as an assembly station for volunteers like Horst and his traveling companions waiting to be sent to Israel. Clearly, they weren't the first group to occupy the premises. They settled in and did more of what they did best, waited. The next day, another group arrived and a week later, another one, and before long there were more than 200 of them waiting.

The group waited while negotiations were going on for a vessel. Each transport depended on the size of the vessel procured. They consisted mainly of fishing vessels of various sizes. Apparently the deal with the last vessel fell through but there was another boat on its way to get them out of there.

Rumors spread that Israel was winning the war and by the time this group got there, the war would be over. Horst didn't know whether the rumors were true or not. As they waited, the deal on the second vessel fell through. The group was told that this time those in control were positive that a ship had been found and that it was on its way to Marseille.

About a month after their arrival, Horst and the others were finally told to pack up as their transportation to "the promised land" had arrived. He is quick to point out:

"Mind you, very few of us had volunteered to go to Israel for religious reasons. Most of us had left what little religion we did have in the death camps a long time ago and the reason for my being here, as so many others like me found out, was strictly that it beat rotting in a DP camp with little hope for anything better to come along." (Stern, 2006)

Finally, a ship was secured. The group had no idea what to expect. They thought perhaps there would be some sort passenger ship waiting for them. They didn't expect to see an ocean liner or anything but they thought there might be a few cabins and portholes with some plumbing. When the truck finally stopped at a small fishing vessel their illusions of a dining room and all the amenities that come with a cruise ship in the Mediterranean were quickly thwarted.

In front of them was a fishing vessel about 60 feet long. It had a wheelhouse and a flat deck with two cargo holds. It appeared that the previous tenants were evacuated to make room for this group and they had obviously left abruptly and hadn't bothered to clean up after themselves before their departure. The smell of fish was overpowering, yet this would be home for the future fighters for the next 12 days.

After Horst and the others boarded the ship, they were divided into two groups. One went into the left cargo hold and the others went to the one on the right. Each hold had platforms that were about six tiers high with just enough room to crawl in and onto a thin mattress to sleep on. The leader told them to make themselves at home so Horst ventured up on deck. After an initial look around he found a spot with enough space located behind a lifeboat out of everyone's way and it became his nook for the duration of the trip.

The crew consisted of four seamen and the captain who kept to themselves. One person told Horst that he couldn't possibly stay in his chosen spot because it could get very uncomfortable in the rain. He assured the man that he was willing to take his chances. The man answered only with, "It's your funeral." He felt that any place was better than where the others ended up in the belly of the boat. As he got comfortable in his little spot he noticed that it was fairly close to the galley which appeared to be little more than a shed. He walked over to it and asked the person in charge for a job helping out in the kitchen.

Horst was given the job and that's where he remained, peeling potatoes, opening cans, and distributing food, for the duration of the trip. He kept so busy that he didn't have time to get seasick but he felt sorry for those in the hold who did. Those who were stuck in the hold lived in cramped conditions and had the stench of fish and many unwashed bodies to contend with. He was glad to stay up top and keep busy.

Some members of the group rigged a few shower stalls but with clean water rationed, they could only shower with salt water. In addition to the rigged showers, latrines were set up at the stern of the ship, two latrines enclosed only by a sheet for over 200 people.

The men often relieved themselves off the side of the boat and the two latrines were left for the women to use.

As soon as they settled in, there was an emergency drill. They were told that they could spend as much time as they wanted on deck but as soon as the alarm sounded, which indicated another ship or a plane had been sighted, they needed to clear the deck immediately. Horst recalls the need to hide.

"The reason for this was that we were running the gauntlet, which the British had set up before the state of Israel was even declared. Any vessel larger than a rowboat caught on the open sea and that looked suspicious of smuggling people into Palestine, was to be boarded and if found carrying any, escorted to the isle of Cyprus and the people to be interned for the duration of the war that raged at the time between Israel and seven Arab countries." (Stern, 2006)

After an 11-day voyage, the group finally reached Israel in the month of August and on the twelfth day they made port at the docks in Haifa. There wasn't much to see, except large storage buildings and in the distance they had a good view of Mount Carmel. Later, it would be Horst's home for a while. It looked like a fair-sized city. Everything seemed quiet, not at all what they expected to see in a port city. It was as if no one was working that day but that was most likely because it was Saturday, the Sabbath.

As the group disembarked, trucks were waiting for them and before they knew it, they were in a tent city somewhere in Israel. A sergeant introduced himself and told us that he was the lucky fellow who was elected by his peers to try and make soldiers out of them. He was a born Israeli, called a sabre from German parentage so he was able to communicate with them in German. First he gave them a command in Hebrew and then repeated it in German. Such as, "Select a cot, put your belongings down and empty all your pockets. Not to worry, no one will steal anything. When you're done, follow me."

The Israeli soldier marched them directly to the showers. No one could blame him. They smelled ripe, this was the first real shower they had seen since they left France and Horst expected that they would clog the drainage system with their filth. While they were in the showers, their clothing disappeared, never to be seen again and the group ended up in a delousing station. After that, they were outfitted from head to toe in uniforms, shoes, and everything else required to make them look like soldiers. From there, they went to eat at the mess hall and finally, they were given rifles.

Finally, Horst and the rest of the group were told to settle in and rest up because the next day those in charge intended to try make soldiers out of them. They learned quickly that this man meant what he said. Awakened at 6 a.m., they were sent to run a mile and back. Then, they were sent to the showers, after which they had to fall in and start marching, as the leader barked, "Left, right, left..." in Hebrew. In the beginning, they looked ridiculous. It took a while, but eventually they eventually marched like real soldiers.

Left: Horst Stern - Israeli Army- Hagana. Right: Horst Stern - Israeli Army - Pal-Mach

Getting up at six in the morning didn't sit well with Horst so when "rise and shine" was called, he came up with the idea of pushing his army cot next to the one he was on. Then he stretched out sideways at the head of it, pulled the blanket over his head and went back to sleep. The sergeant just made a cursory inspection so he got away with it for the first week. Boot camp was a three-week training program and in that time they learned how to march. Finally, day that they had all been waiting for arrived. They were taken to the shooting range and each one of them received ten bullets for his rifle. Ammunition was scarce but they were still challenged to see who the best shooter was.

There were targets in the distance. Horst didn't know how far away they were but there were six of them so six of them took aim and fired at the same time. Rumor had it that they were looking for sharpshooters and it was common knowledge that the life expectancy of a sharpshooter was short. Horst hit what he wanted to hit and all except one of his shots went where he intended them to go but that didn't mean that he missed the target completely, the bullet hit the frame that held the target. The next stage of training as a soldier was crucial, learning to throw a hand grenade. The instructor demonstrated how to do it right but cautioned, "If you do it wrong, you don't have to worry about it. Either it is the end of you, or you become a veteran, might even get a medal for stupidity." Fortunately, all the grenades the recruits threw were dummies. He now quips, "like us."

For the final stage of their training, they were taken out on a march one night in full gear, minus ammunition of course, and about five kilometers from camp, they were told to pair up wait five minutes and then try to find their way back to camp.

It was on that dark, moonless, night with visibility of about five feet that Horst first realized he had no sense of direction, a problem he's still plagued with today. Luckily for him though, he was paired with someone who he refers to as a night owl. He knew exactly where to go and they were back at camp in record time. Everyone reached camp safely, there were only a few stragglers. There was no ceremony or fanfare. They were simply told that they had all passed the course and were declared certified soldiers of the Haganah, and as such, they were ready for anything. Following the announcement, they were put into an elite unit called the Palmach. The group proudly wore the unit's camel emblem on their jackets, even though they hadn't earned it yet.

Some big names served in and made the Palmach what it was,

such as, Yigal Allon, Moshe Dayan, Yitzhak Rabin, Uzu Narkiss, and Ezer Weitzmann. Then a bunch of German Jews came along with hardly any training, who had never seen any action, and they got to join the Palmach. They didn't know it at the time but the war would end soon and they were fortunate to never really come face to face with the enemy. The few times they saw them, they were already dead. He shares an example of what little action they saw:

"Our platoon, if you want to call it that, was sent to the Negev to take the town of Beer-Sheba, but by the time we had arrived, all we could see were a few dead Arabs laying on the road, and entering cautiously some of their houses, all we did find was that the food was still warm on the table, suggesting that the inhabitants did leave in a hurry. Seemed that the real Palmach paved the way for us to go in. Turned out the whole town was abandoned, not a soul to be seen, not even a dog." (Stern, 2006)

Luckily for the group, the residents didn't have time to booby trap any of the houses. If they were, there would have been many casualties because they had no training to recognize or much less disarm them. They also didn't have any training in house-to-house fighting. They moved into the houses after giving them a thorough clean, despite having to haul water from a well because of the lack of any running water, and after the dust settled they just gave up and slept.

There was also no electric light in their new home so they used kerosene lamps that the former inhabitants had left behind. Although they made use of these necessities, they didn't find anything of value. The former inhabitants had taken their most prized possessions with them as they fled. The only things they left behind were a few chickens, a bunch of pigeons flying around town and some donkeys.

Living there was easy with very little for them to do. Horst always traveled without some reading material so he didn't get bored. Before long though, they were informed by their superiors that there was some trouble with the food supply line and there were only enough provisions for three or four days. They were told to see if they could scrounge up something to eat themselves. There was enough flour around for fresh bread plus some vegetables but the main courses would have to be supplied on their own and that was easier said than done.

The eight residents of the house decided to go out in pairs to try and secure some food. On their first excursion they were able to corner three chickens but none of the soldiers from their house could bring themselves to kill an innocent animal. Horst finally volunteered to do the deed. One man got water from the well, another guy lit the stove, and someone found a pot big enough to hold the three chickens. They also scavenged some vegetables and seasoning. Even though there were only three chickens and eight of them, with the bread they had they were able to fill up for that day but for the next couple of days, the meals were meager. Their stomachs growled as, apparently, the rest of the chickens in town must have found their way into one pot or another. That's when they resorted to shooting down pigeons.

Almost a week had gone by without provisions coming in and with desperation setting in, they finally decided that they had to kill one of the donkeys. Again, Horst was elected as hunter, butcher and chef and suddenly he had to justify his decision to make a stew. Some of the other men whined,

"Why can't we have some steaks?"

"Who elected you to decide what to cook?"

That's when Horst told them that they had a choice, "Take it, or leave it," followed by, "better yet, go and kill your own donkey." When he asked them if any of them had ever eaten horsemeat, none answered. He told them that he had eaten horsemeat after he came out of the ghetto and that it was tougher than shoe leather. So, it soon came to be that all the men satiated themselves on donkey stew.

Soon after that, the field kitchen got reestablished and they no longer had to worry about where their next meal would come from, which was fortunate, Horst felt that the only living things, besides people, left in Beer-Sheba were flies and bugs. They had eaten everything else.

Out of the blue, the platoon got a three-day pass to go anywhere they wanted. Horst chose to hitchhike to Tel Aviv where he went to the beach and looked up some relatives he hadn't met before, "Those were the ones smart enough to get out of Germany before the crap hit the fan."

Horst was disappointed that he didn't connect with any of them. He said that they were very polite but were clearly uninterested in his visit. "Oh yes, you are the son of Erna? Well, it was nice meeting you. Drop by again the next time you are in town." Horst realized that it also might have been his own fault. He was too shy and still stuttered, which made him self-conscious.

Horst moved on and found a bookstore with some German books for sale, so he purchased six of them and hitchhiked back to Beer-Sheba. He was happy and enjoyed a good time with his new friends. With the next day came the news that they would be replacing another platoon that had been guarding the town. After reaching the spot, they doubled up and took over the foxholes that were already in place. Every day was the same.

The only excitement they had was that after everybody had settled down and all was quiet; the guards had been posted for the night when one of them opened fire. Naturally, everybody woke up and jumped into position. Horst grabbed his rifle too and without seeing a thing, they all started shooting. They had no idea what to expect after they were finally told to cease fire.

The morning light brought humiliation. Once it got light enough to see, they were anxious to determine how many of the enemy they had killed, they ventured out but all they could detect was a big lump in the distance. After closer inspection, it turned out to be a cow. When the guard who had started the entire ruckus was asked what made him open fire, he replied that he detected movement in the distance and after challenging whatever it was, and not even receiving a moo in return, he opened fire.

After spending the next three weeks there, the platoon was finally replaced. They left Beer-Sheba and after driving around the Negev for a while, they ended up at a large stone fort with walls at least two feet thick and quite old, by the looks of it. One memory stands out of his time there. One day, while on patrol, they encountered some Arab sheep herders surrounded by at least 60 sheep and goats. The lieutenant, who spoke fluent Arabic, spoke to the two men and the result of the conversation was that the platoon took custody of the sheep and goats and herded the flock of animals back into the fort. Horst couldn't see if any money was exchanged during this transaction, but he saw the two herders sent on their way.

Horst was elected butcher again and he killed two of the animals a day and for doing so he was excused from going on patrol. For the next month, they ate meat every day. The day finally arrived when they were replaced at the fort and they went back to the headquarters, where they originally came from.

Once back at headquarters Horst was called in by the commander of the fort and asked if he would like to work in the kitchen. This was an unexpected request and Horst asked him if this was punishment, he couldn't recall having done anything that would warrant it. The commander smiled and explained that he was told that Horst was good worker at the fort and that this was kind of a promotion, if he wanted to take the job. Remembering all the years of hunger, his brain went into overdrive and he jumped at the opportunity. There was another reason Horst took the cooking job.

"I hated everything pertaining to the army, the marching, the discipline, the slow destruction of one's inner self, to robotize one into a killing machine. I do realize that to be a warrior you have to give up a lot of your humanity but I was not ready to do that again. I just went through one hell, and I was not quite ready yet to enter another one." (Stern, 2006)

The first six months were filled with peeling potatoes, various other vegetables, and cooking meals in industrial-sized pots and pans, almost as large as a bath tub, for at least 1000 men.

"That was a lot of bellies to feed and eggs to crack and I had lost my butcher status for I was never asked again to butcher anything bigger than an egg." (Stern, 2006)

Horst considered this job a dream come true. He worked for two days and had two days off. He found it to be fun but with such a light schedule he decided to find an outside job to supplement his army income. One morning, on his day off, Horst walked to the farm country, which was about three miles from camp. Upon closer inspection, he discovered about a dozen small collective farms around the camp. He learned that they were individually run and managed but the heavy equipment was jointly owned.

When Horst reached the third house, he found success. The farmer spoke fluent German, having left Germany long before Hitler came into power and when Horst told him that he was looking for a job and was available, explaining to him his schedule of work hours at the army camp, the man told him that would be fine with him. He also told Horst that he could begin work right away if he wanted him to. He looked at the uniform Horst was wearing and told him that he had some work clothes for him to change into. There was a whole row of chicken coops, which were built about three feet off the ground and Horst was told to rake and clean underneath them and to collect the debris in burlap bags. He thinks the bags were then sold as fertilizer. When he went under the coops, the smell of ammonia hit him like a ton of bricks. He asked for, and received, a cloth to put over his nose and mouth, which didn't do as much to kill the smell as he had hoped. From there, he learned to do a variety of other jobs on the farm. He was even invited to spend the night in the guest room when he worked consecutive days.

Martin, a friend of Horst's, soon confided in him that he was seriously thinking of getting out of Israel once he got discharged from the army. The chance of anyone of military-serving age getting an exit visa was unlikely. As both Horst and Martin were of military-serving age and "seasoned-trained warriors," the chances of being re-inducted, if the need arose, was almost certain. Neither of them could see a future for themselves there and they were almost certain that the hostilities would continue for a long time to come. After discussing it for days on end, Martin came up with the bright idea of changing their religion and becoming Christians. Horst figured that considering who his parents were he was already halfway there and Martin's situation was similar.

Little did they know that at that time there were thousands of volunteers of all nationalities and religions fighting for the Israelis. Those were professional soldiers, experts in the art of war. Some fought for the money but most of them, Horst learned later, for ideological reasons.

The farmer Horst worked for had to let him go because he caught up with his workload but asked him to check in with him in a month or so. By that time, he was sure that there would be enough work again for a few days. This was the break Horst was hoping for. Martin and Horst worked out a plan to begin switching religions and after much conversation, they both agreed that the best place to find a mission looking for converts would be in Jerusalem. After hitching their way there, the first mission they came upon was called the Bible Evangelistic Mission. As they walked into the chapel, they were greeted by an English man who turned out to be the pastor. He resided there with his wife and two children.

Martin acted as the spokesman for the duo because his English was better than Horst's and even with the few English words Horst knew, he still stuttered although not as badly as he used to. However, he remained self-conscious of it. Martin told the pastor that there was something missing in their lives and after having read the Bible they thought that this might be what they were searching for. Martin must have made a good case because the pastor agreed to show them the way to eternal happiness and informed them that after they went through certain rituals and proved that they were ready to enter the faith, he would grant their conversion request if he decided that they passed.

"*There was a lot of mumble-jumble and none of it made much sense to me but what the hell? It worked. We both had a good time while staying with the padre. He fed us, he put us up for the nights, and he even showed us Jerusalem. He drove us all around, and it did not cost us a penny.*" (Stern, 2006)

Horst didn't learn much about religion but his English definitely improved during his stay at the mission. The people were very nice to him and Martin and it only took them four sessions before they were deemed worthy of Baptism. Horst had a sneaking suspicion that the pastor couldn't afford to feed them anymore , they ate him out of house and home. The two young men appreciated the change in menu from their usual fare.

For the event of the baptism the church was packed to capacity. There was a sunken tub, usually hidden beneath the floorboards, which was uncovered and filled with hip-deep water for the occasion. As Horst entered the water, everybody was chanting and before he knew what was happening to him the minister had ahold of him by the neck and the chest. Water rushed over him as he was swiftly dunked and nearly drowned. Martin's turn followed with the same flourish and near drowning. After the dunking, the pastor told them that there was some genuine water from the Jordan mixed with the rest of the water and that they were special for that particular reason. This meant nothing to Horst. He didn't know then, and still doesn't know now, what the significance was.

There was a celebration following the ceremony. The pastor celebrated saving two more lost souls who were officially half Jewish and half Christian but who turned away from their Judaism to embrace the Christian faith fully. Horst felt that they both put on an Oscar-worthy performance that day. Horst returned to his old working schedule in the kitchen and on his days off he went back to the farm. Clearly, in the kitchen, they were satisfied with his work because upon his return he was told to see the chef in his office. There, the chef proposed that the army wanted to send him to a cooking school. They had watched him work and felt he would make a good cook. This also meant there would be some sergeant stripes in it for him, better pay, and a good future in the army. Horst respectfully declined the offer and told the chef that he was perfectly happy with the way things were but would think about the offer and would let him know if he changed his mind.

20

THE REUNION

About a year had passed since Horst arrived in Israel, he was biding his time and trying to stay out of trouble. He realized that he had another year of service ahead of him before he could even think about a discharge from the army. By then, he hoped he would have a different perspective and an idea of what he wanted out of life. Worrying about his future was futile, though. It was out of his hands as Mother Nature had a plan that completely differed from any plan he had intended for himself.

About two weeks after he turned down the promotion and after returning from his four-day working vacation on the farm, one of his buddies entered his room and informed him that that the commander wanted to see him "on the double." Wondering what he had done this time, he wracked his brain but couldn't remember involvement in any recent wrongdoings. He thought that perhaps it had something to do with the job promotion. He rushed over to find out and put his mind at rest. Upon entering, he was immediately told to sit down and Horst feared bad news would soon follow.

The officer in charge rose from the desk and waved a sheet of paper in the air. The officer addressed him as Private Zwei, Horst realized, "The name Horst, which I had successfully used for 20 years, couldn't be translated into Hebrew, so they changed it to Zwei." The officer went on to tell Horst he was a lucky man. He had just learned that Horst's mother and grandmother had arrived in Israel a week before and were having difficulty finding a Horst Stern. Finally, a bureaucrat suggested that there may have been a name change and that they had a Zwie Stern and found where he was stationed.

Furthermore, he was informed that his leave would be extended indefinitely so he could join the family in the tent city near Haifa where they were temporarily housed. The officer handed him his papers and wished him luck.

"*All I could say was shit. I was dumbfounded, and I thought that a mistake had been made. I could not believe that Erna would pull a stunt like that, especially after I had sent her numerous letters explaining the situation there in Israel, and whatever she should decide, Israel should be out of the question.*" (Stern, 2006)

Horst said his goodbyes in camp, packed up what little belongings he had, and asked Martin to do him a favor and go see his farmer friend to explain the situation. As it turned out, Martin continued working for the farmer after Horst's departure for quite a while, which made Horst feel like something good came out of the whole mess after all.

After about six hours of hitchhiking, Horst arrived at the camp. The sight that met him was pitiful. They were housed in a huge army tent that accommodated about 40 people. Amongst the sea of people, he finally found them sitting on army cots on a sand floor with suitcases as a table. When Selma saw him her face lit up and for just a moment he forgot how angry he was at Erna for putting her mother through all this hardship.

Both women were so happy to see Horst and he reluctantly admitted that he was just as happy to see them. After the hugs and kisses were over, he asked his mother just one question. Why? Of all of the places on Earth, and after all the letters he had written to her explaining the situation in Israel, why would they go there? The only answer he received was that they had missed him, especially his grandmother. Horst says that the statement took the "wind out of my sails, and what more could I say?" Selma and Erna had been in such a hurry to see him that they traveled by airplane.

Horst learned that some of the people in the tent had been waiting for a month for permanent housing. With the influx of people arriving in the country, they were behind in finding suitable housing for all of them. They had no choice but to wait, patiently, for the housing situation to be solved.

What Horst didn't know was that Selma had found out, through her daughter Rosa in Berlin, that Selma's nephew, Alex, and his wife, who wasn't Jewish, survived the war. They had been bombed out three times. Alex had also gotten divorced and remarried a woman who was half-Jewish. They went on to have a child and immigrated to Israel.

Erna wrote to him to let him know that they arrived in Israel and would like to see him. It didn't take Alex and his family long to appear and when they saw the conditions in which they were living, the couple invited them to stay at their home without hesitation. Horst had arrived just in time to help them move.

Alex and his wife, Lore, had been fortunate, there were plenty of apartments available in Haifa when they arrived. Apparently when Haganah took the city during the war, many of the inhabitants packed up whatever they could carry and left the city in a hurry. The vacated apartments were assigned to the newcomers. Alex's family received a one-bedroom apartment with a huge living room, a kitchen and a bathroom in the center of Haifa.

Horst wondered where he would spend the night, It was already late afternoon by the time they moved and settled in, and he suddenly got really sick. He couldn't function well at all and the pain in his stomach was so bad that the rest of the family decided to call an ambulance, which took him to the nearest army hospital.

Once at the hospital, he was given shots to help ease the pain. The doctor wanted to know if he had ever had this kind of problem before. He told him that he got stomach pains when he was young and that hot water bottles would sometimes help. For the next few days, he was poked and prodded. He also had to drink some "awful-tasting stuff," was x-rayed and was put on a diet. He was in there for two weeks and the doctors couldn't find a cause for his problems but he said they were the most peaceful weeks that he was able to enjoy for a long time to come.

Following his release from the hospital, Horst was informed that he had been discharged from the army. As he was now the sole provider for his family, the army classified his as a hardship case. There was one stipulation to his release. Every three months, he had to report to the army post for reserve duty. He admits that he didn't fulfill this requirement and no one tried very hard to find him and make him report either.

Horst discovered that there was a downside to his new situation. Every civilian citizen of Israel received a food ration card, which guaranteed access to hard-to-come-by items like eggs, meat, butter, and chicken, depending on the supply to stores from the government. Most of the items could be bought on the black market but the prices were outrageous. Since Horst wasn't registered he had to do without a few things but they managed to get by somehow.

While Horst was in the hospital, his mother found a place for the three of them to live. Alex, whom they had been staying with, started a plumbing business that he ran from his apartment. He ended up doing a job for a man who owned a big house on the Carmel, in Haifa. When Alex mentioned that his cousin was looking for a place for herself and her mother, he mentioned that he had a room in his house and told Alex to send her up to take a look at it.

With the flood of immigrants at that time, rentals were at a premium so naturally Horst turned over all of the money he had saved to help pay for whatever came along. Besides, he knew that Alex and his wife would be happy to get their place back to themselves. After all, there were five of them staying in one room, now six with Horst out of the hospital, and a dog. Horst says that he never forgot their kindness, taking them in when they needed it.

Giving up his savings left Horst broke but at least he had a place to go once he was released from the hospital. When he entered his new lodgings, it place took his breath away. The house was a two-story building with walls at least 18 inches thick, standing in a garden-like setting. He couldn't help thinking about how different this was from where they had come from in the Budapest Ghetto. Now, they were living in the best neighborhood in Haifa.

The area of the home in which they lived was actually down in the cellar. The room was about 144 square feet and he was fascinated with the ceiling, which was a bit over eight feet high at its highest point, made completely of brick and oval in shape. However, the floor was sand. After digging a hole about three feet deep, he found nothing but sand and Horst convinced himself that it was genuinely beach sand, and that he was living on the beach.

Three army cots lined the walls and there was a bar-like structure made out of concrete blocks. There was a faucet with running, cold, water and a drain. From the ceiling, hung a single-bulbed light fixture with a pull chain. There weren't any windows, only the entry door. The bathrooms and showers were on the floor above and they shared with many others living in the house. Horst described the rest of the furnishings like this:

"In a way, it was a step up on life's ladder. In Budapest, we had to go downstairs to go to use the toilet, and there were no showers. After, I was able to scrounge up some wooden boxes, so we had more room to put in some of the stuff we had kept in our suitcases. Almost forgot, this penthouse also came with a table and two chairs. I used my bed to sit on. There was also a small dresser and some homemade shelves." (Stern, 2006)

Selma did all the cooking for the trio. The concrete bar doubled as a platform where they had a "Primo stove-like contraption" that worked like a camp stove, fueled by kerosene and a little plunger that pumped air into the cylinder. They referred to it as a pressure cooker. Horst's grandmother produced some wonderful meals on this makeshift stove. He never understood how those two women could put so many delicious meals on the table, having so little to work with.

There was never a shortage of frozen fish. It was one of the few items that they didn't have to have a ration stamp to get. For quite some time, he ate fish so often that he thought he was actually growing fins.

Erna took a job as a cook in a small restaurant in downtown Haifa. The only job Horst could find was at a motorcycle shop that specialized in adding sidecars to regular motorcycles. At least it was close to where they lived. However, after about a month of doing nothing but clean motorcycles, he decided to make a change.

In retrospect, had Horst kept that job, he might have turned into a pretty good mechanic but instead he chose a job in construction. The year was 1949 and he felt there must have been a lot of money floating around because buildings were springing up all over town. The buildings being erected ranged from big private homes to condos and apartments. Helping to build them was hard work but at least this time he was getting paid for his efforts.

Following the progress of each project that he worked on and helping on each construction site brought great satisfaction to Horst. He learned a lot about construction by asking many questions. Fortunately, the foreman had the patience to answer most of them. He stayed with that job until the day he left Haifa. The pay was good and it was a Monday to Friday job. That didn't mean he rested on the weekends, though.

Erna found jobs for both her and Horst at an open-aired coffee house around the corner from where they lived, and his weekends were spent working there. Situated in a gardenlike atmosphere with tables set up under the shade of the trees, they were actually able to take Selma with them. They sat her in a shady spot and let her order whatever she wanted. Although the menu was limited they served items such as coffee, cake, and ice cream topped with exotic liquors served in tall glasses. There was also the option of beer or wine. Selma enjoyed the cake and coffee as Erna worked in the kitchen and because Horst had picked up enough of the language, he took the orders. The pay was minimal but the tips made it worth it.

Before they realized it, a year had passed. Horst and Erna had spoken about their situation in Israel and she finally realized that what he said in his letters was true. It was dangerous for her and

Selma. So, Erna applied for an exit visa for both of them and eventually it was granted, mainly due to Selma's age and the circumstances under which they had to live. Horst, however, still being of military age, stood next to no chance of getting a visa to leave the country, at least not for a while.

21

GOODBYE LADIES

By the time the exit visas came, the family had saved enough money to book one-way tickets to Germany for Erna and Selma. They would stop in Marseille and then they would travel by train all the way to Munich. Erna had kept in touch with some of the people in the camp where she and Selma had stayed before they flew to Israel. They told her that there were still people living in DP camps and there was still a chance to immigrate to America and Canada. That was good news to the trio because they had their doubts. Horst's mother and grandmother left with a promise to do whatever they could to secure an exit visa for him as well. After he saw them off, he returned to the now lonely and eerie cellar.

It was too quiet in the cellar as Horst lay on his cot and took stock of his life and everything that had happened up to that point. Even after the war ended in 1945, he had been on one adventure after another in Budapest. From 1946 to 1948, he had been in DP camps in Austria and Germany and then he spent 1948 to 1951 in Israel "dodging bullets once again." Now Erna and Selma were off to Germany and eventually, Canada. As sad as he was to be without them, he knew it was a step in the right direction.

As he spent time alone in the dark cellar, his mind drifted back to nights spent on the cot when his family was still together. He would ask his grandmother to recite some of the poems she had memorized as a child. Over 80 years old and her memory was phenomenal. Even now, all these years later when he thinks about those times, it brings tears to his eyes.

Six months passed and Horst "worked his butt off." Once in a while some of his old army friends would come and stay with him for a few days. He also continued to work weekends at the coffee house. One Saturday, during a lull in business, he met a lady and her ten-year-old son and they struck up a conversation.

The woman, Lea, and her husband had emigrated there from Germany back in the 1930s. Both were Zionists and lived in a kibbutz for a while. They ended up divorcing and she remarried another German Jew in Israel, but unfortunately he died in his sleep before he reached 50. Horst explained his Germany connection and that he had just sent his mother and grandmother back there, he continued working construction during the week and at the coffee house on weekends until he had the opportunity to join them.

Lea then told him that the superintendent of the apartment house where she lived was looking for someone who wasn't afraid to get his hands dirty and the money would be very good. He couldn't resist and went to the address she gave him. He spoke with the super and was told that the job consisted of cleaning out a huge septic tank built out of bricks with weep holes all around it. It was about ten feet in diameter and 12 feet deep. The hole was loaded with big rocks that had to be taken out, washed, and stacked. Then, once they were all removed and cleaned, they needed to be thrown back in. He told Host that the tank had been out of service for quite a while, so the odor wouldn't be too bad.

Horst almost couldn't keep a straight face, the pay rate was quoted stunned him. He was offered more money than he would make in a month at the construction job. Although he could only work weekends the man agreed and Horst set out to find someone to help him because it was definitely going to be a two-man job.

Fortunately, Horst kept in touch with Martin, who had left so abruptly when he was mustered out of the army. Martin passed messages along to him from the farmer who he had worked for, Horst replied and said that if Martin was ever in Haifa to look him up. As Horst arrived home from work one night, he found Martin sitting outside his door waiting for him to return. The two of them spent some time catching up. Unfortunately, Martin had no idea how to get out of the situation he was in.

Martin informed Horst that he was on a ten-day leave from the army so Horst asked if he'd like to make some good money and told him about the job, which would be a "stinker," pun intended. He offered to split the money equally as he didn't want to take advantage of his friend.

Horst took three days leave from the construction job and he and Martin went to work. It was a nasty job but the two young men worked well together. The only thing he liked about the job was that it paid well. Also, Lea, the woman who got them the job, brought them lunch and cold drinks every day. They finished the job within a week and just in time as Martin's leave came to an end. After dividing the pay, Martin left with a smile on his face. Unfortunately, they lost contact. Horst never heard from him again but looks back and hopes Martin became a singer. He had a beautiful voice.

One night, after the job was finished, Lea invited Henry over for dinner and because he hadn't eaten a home-cooked meal since his mother and grandmother left, he graciously accepted. Lea lived within walking distance to Horst's apartment and on the walk there he stopped and bought some flowers for her.

Horst and Lea hit it off. They talked for hours and about so many things. She was a pretty woman and fluent in three languages. When he asked her if she would teach him English, her reply was simply, "We shall see." Before he knew it, almost half of the night was gone. He reluctantly said good bye but promised to call on her again soon. With that, their friendship began.

During the day, Lea ran a kindergarten out of her home and when she asked Horst to build a sandbox out of cinderblocks for the children one day, he happily obliged. The two began spending more time together and Lea showed him all of the good things in life. They went to concerts, the opera, and had some field trips to Bethlehem. They would even go swim in the Galilee. They had a great time together. Despite it all their relationship remained platonic, even though Horst eventually fell in love with her.

At the time, Haifa didn't have an opera house and everything pertaining to art was presented in people's private homes. Together Horst and Lea attended quite a few of these gatherings. He still remembers her fondly for introducing him to all of the beauty life has to offer.

Meanwhile, Erna had been sending letters to Horst and she informed him that she had finally found a job in Munich. She worked in an office that handled restitution for people who survived the horrors of the Hitler Regime. She and Selma rented an apartment there that was leased by the IRO. The house in which it was located was available especially for the elderly and they qualified because of Selma's age.

Erna explained that she had put in a petition to the Israeli government for an exit visa for Horst on the grounds that he was the main provider for her and her mother. It took a while, but eventually he was granted the exit visa, something he says that was like winning the lottery. Israel needed every able-bodied person at that time. He had never heard of anyone else, at least not the guys that he had gone there with, who made it back.

With all of the necessary paperwork in his possession, Horst packed his belongings and said his good byes to the few people he knew. The most difficult one was Lea. As much as he was in love with her, his love to get out of Israel was greater.

22

BACK TO EUROPE

Horst boarded the TSS Kedma to journey back to Europe. A journey that had taken him 11 days in a fishing boat, took only four on the return trip. He arrived in Marseille where he then boarded a train to Italy. He decided to play tourist for a day in Milan and he fondly remembers a cathedral there with its breathtaking beauty as a masterpiece of architecture. He then continued on to Germany by train.

Within a week of being in Munich, Horst discovered that he wasn't welcome to stay in the apartment as it was primarily a home for the elderly and his being there was against the rules. Therefore, the three Sterns moved to another DP camp in Wolfratshausen. It was about 30 kilometers from Munich. It was déjà vu as they found themselves in a familiar scenario; army cots and sharing a room. This time though, they took in a boarder. Erna and Horst got Selma a dog, named Molly, to keep her company while they worked.

Horst started working as a driver for the Hebrew Immigrant Aid Society, where his mother also worked and the place that would play a major role in their future. Unfortunately, he had misplaced his driver's license but he had another one reissued in Munich so he was able to drive. The main problem was that he had trouble finding his way around because he had never lived in Munich before. He eventually overcame the challenge and everything worked out.

By 1951, the Sterns were back to square one. The past five years hadn't been easy and were, in fact, somewhat interesting. They had seen and survived a lot, including another war. Yet, if someone was to ask Horst if he would do it all again, his answer would be, "Of course I would." Admittedly though, he learned what not to do in the future. He soon realized that staying in Germany was out of the question. The wounds were just too deep.

Securing a visa to the United States didn't look promising. Their strict policies made it nearly impossible. They thought of Canada but he knew so little about it. He envisioned a frozen wasteland with nothing but snow and ice. For the time being though, they continued where they were and dealt with it the best they could.

Driving for a living in the city of Munich, Horst came into contact with many Germans, which was new for him. He hadn't had much direct contact with any since leaving Berlin. Even there, he had led quite a sheltered life. Other than a few Fräuleins, he hardly had any contact with the German population. In Munich, it was different. They rode the train with them and talked openly about the war with them. Most of them claimed to have hated the war years but a few die-hards said that, given the chance, they would vote Hitler right back into office.

The next six months passed quickly and uneventfully except for occasional rumors that most people ignored. Horst fell in love again with a young lady who worked in one of the offices at work and during this affair, his absence meant that Erna had to take the train to work by herself. I will spare you from his, quite colorful, version of what led to the end of this whirlwind love affair after only three weeks but instead will inform you that it was a mutual parting.

When Erna first arrived from Israel, she registered the three of them at the HIAS for emigration. When she was asked if she had any preference as to where she would like to emigrate she simply told them she'd be happy with any place that was out of Germany, with the exception of the Balkan countries or Russia. After providing the necessary information about Horst and Selma, she was told that their chances were slim as Selma was already 85 years old, but they would try.

So much time had passed that they had honestly forgotten about emigrating until one night when Horst and Erna returned home from work and Selma handed them a letter from the very place they worked for, HIAS. Erna opened and read it aloud. It stated that if they were still interested in emigrating, Canada had increased the quota of refugees that it was willing to accept. They could go to the offices to fill out the necessary paper work.

After little sleep, the Sterns were the first to arrive at the offices the next morning to fill out and turn in the paperwork. They tried not to get their hopes up. After all, the process had begun five years ago and there they were, still. They went back to their daily routines but then two weeks later, to their surprise, they received a message to report for an interview.

People had told them that their chances of being accepted were slim due to Selma's age and it would be risky for her to deal with the rigors of the trip. Yet, they were informed that they had "almost been accepted," and that it would all depend on their last interview, if they were selected for one, with the Canadian Consul. They would be notified in time. Horst thought, *here we go again.*

Looking back, they should've been more optimistic because three weeks later they received a notice in the mail to be at a certain place for another interview, only this time it was actually with the Canadian Consul. They had to travel by train to attend the meeting which was held in another DP camp, a non-Jewish camp filled with people of mixed nationalities. He doesn't recall the name of the town or the camp.

Upon their arrival, they were given a room and told to settle in because it might take a couple of days before they were called in for an interview. They were used to waiting. It was now March, 1952, and they had been waiting since 1946. This camp was different from the ones they had previously been in. What stood out most to Horst was that there were hardly any elderly people or children to be seen.

The camp was filled, mostly, with young men from the Scandinavian and Balkan countries. Most were in their twenties and from Yugoslavia, Poland, Hungary, Romania, and the Ukraine. They soon learned that these people couldn't return to their countries because they were considered fugitives, they had supported the wrong side, Hitler's, during the war. Their collaboration with the enemy meant that in returning home there would be consequences like long prison terms or hangings.

These men had volunteered to fight on the German side during the war and quite a few joined the SS to actively take part in the atrocities that had been perpetrated. These were the people the Sterns had to compete with for entry permits to Canada. For years after, it made Horst sick to think back on seeing "those scum" coming out from their interviews with the consul. They had big smiles on their faces and would mouth the words, "I got it." It angers him that they never had to pay for the crimes they committed against humanity. Horst honestly believes that while they waited for their interview, the ration of visas was at least seven to three in favor of the non-Jews.

When at last they were called in for their interview they were told that their papers all appeared to be in order. There was one stipulation though. They had to sign a document, agreeing, that when they arrived in Montreal, because of their age, Selma would go into a nursing home arranged by the HIAS. They talked it over and it took them all of about three minutes to agree to those terms. Erna and Horst figured that they would just cross that bridge when they got to it. The consul said that this was a first for him as he shook their hands and wished them luck.

From then on, everything went smoothly. As directed, they packed their luggage and boarded a bus that would take them to the train station. From there, they boarded the train for Bremerhaven where they were to board a ship that would take them to Halifax, Canada.

Once onboard the ship, Horst was directed towards the steerage section to share a cabin with seven other men. Erna and Selma were given an outside cabin with a porthole view and its own bathroom. As the ship got underway, he stood at the railing and watched the country, that had brought so much hardship and death to so many people, disappear. As he wondered what was in store for them on this new continent, he started to feel really good and grateful for another chance to try again. They wanted to go to America but at least this was the first phase. After all, Canada was on the North American continent.

The food onboard the ship was quite good and the trip was pleasant. Halfway to their destination, however, they ran into what Horst considered "a hell of a storm." Someone said that the winds were hurricane strength. Personally, all he was able to observe was that the bow of the ship disappeared one moment and the next moment, it reappeared. It shot high into the air and the next moment went back under again. One had to hold on for dear life or be prepared to swim the rest of the way. People didn't see each other for days because most remained in their cabins throughout the storm. Erna, Selma, and Horst, though, had the dining room to themselves.

Eleven days after setting sail to cross the Atlantic, they finally docked in Halifax. It was a memorable day because it was his 24th birthday, April 8, 1952. It had taken them six long years to realize their dream of setting foot onto the North American continent. Disembarkment went smoothly. All they had to do was show their immigration papers. Soon after they were checked and stamped, they were on a bus heading for the train station. On the ride there, Horst thought, *so, this is Canada! Here I come. Show me what you got.*

23

OH CANADA!

Horst thought about those six years as he rode the train. How nice would it be to, finally, live a life free of fear and persecution for one's religious beliefs or lack thereof? He had felt the same when he arrived in Israel but there was still too much hatred. He realized that there was too much hatred all around the world, despite all that is taught to us.

The train ride to Montreal passed the city of Quebec and took close to 36 hours. By the time they reached their destination, Horst said, "Our butts had calluses from those wooden benches on the train." He felt fortunate though, that it wasn't 100 years earlier when it would've taken them a month to make the trip. Upon their arrival in Montreal, they were welcomed by a woman with the HIAS. She then escorted them to a small hotel where two rooms had been reserved for them. They were told to relax for a couple of days and then someone would call on them to help them get situated.

The HIAS representative handed them an envelope and informed them that there was $60 inside for incidentals and asked them to make it last. They were also given vouchers to a local restaurant where they could get three meals a day. With that, she departed.

There was one other topic the woman brought up before she left. She reminded them that they would have to take Selma to a nursing home as agreed during their interview. The people who ran the nursing home were expecting them that same day. She assured them that it was a nice place where all her needs would be taken care of and where she would be with others her own age who also spoke German or Yiddish. It all sounded pretty good to Horst and Erna but Selma hadn't said a word. Finally, she looked at them and said, "Let's go and get this over with." They piled in the woman's car and she drove them to the home where his grandmother would live out her the remainder of her life.

They stopped in front of a three-story house, not far from the hotel. After climbing about a dozen steps to the entrance door and ringing the doorbell, an elderly woman opened the door and invited them into the home. Following a conversation between the woman driving them and the woman in charge of the nursing home, papers were exchanged, the tour began.

Selma would share a room with another woman, who at that time was in the dining room for dinner with all the other residents. The room was quite nice with two beds with plenty of room between them. The woman in charge asked Selma if she had eaten yet, she said that she wasn't hungry, only tired and really wanted to go to bed after her long day. The suitcases were left packed and once Selma assured them that she would be alright for the night, Erna and Horst promised to return in the morning to help her settle in. Still, they couldn't bring themselves to look her in the eye as they said goodnight and quickly left.

On the way back to the hotel, Horst and his mother had little to say to one another. They both felt like they had just committed a crime. When they finally looked at each other, they knew they were thinking the same thing. Finally, they verbalized it, "No way! Let's go back and get Oma out of there!" They had made it this far together. They could go all the way. They hadn't survived all of those years just to dump Selma at an old age home for convenience.

Finding the house again in the dark proved challenging but

when they found it at last, they rang the doorbell and were greeted by the same woman as earlier. They explained to her that they had made a huge mistake and had come to make it right. The woman didn't know what to think other than it was highly irregular. She suggested that they return in the morning, after having time to think it over. She informed them that if they chose to take Selma out of the home, they'd have to sign a release form so if anything should happen to Selma, she wouldn't be held responsible. Horst requested the papers right there and then and signed them immediately.

After the formalities were over, she escorted them back to the room where Selma was settled in bed. Her eyes were wide open and she looked at them, quizzically. They asked her if she wanted to stay there or return with them. Horst had never seen his grandmother move so fast. With the speed and agility of a 16 year old girl and eyes sparkling with new life, Selma got dressed in record time. Horst picked her suitcase up, which hadn't even been opened yet and they got out of there as quickly as possible, fearing that the lady in charge might change her mind and try to stop them.

They splurged for a taxi to return to the hotel and upon arriving, Selma declared that now she was hungry. Suddenly, they realized that in all the excitement, none of them had eaten in a very long time. They decided to stop at one of the cheaper restaurants. Once back at the hotel, Erna and Selma went to bed and for the first time in years they didn't have to share one. For the first time in ten years, Horst had his own bed and bath. Things were definitely improving.

The following day, the Sterns went to the HAIS office where they were given addresses for places renting rooms, monthly. The first one they visited was in a very nice neighborhood in Montreal. It was owned by a Jewish family with two children. They rented a room and the children took an immediate liking to Selma, who soon became a substitute grandmother to them. Horst settled for a small room with a different family about three blocks away but joined them for most of their evening meals. His grandmother was happy here because they were often together and she was able to cook meals like she used to, this place included kitchen privileges. Erna and Selma even had their own bathroom there. The organization offered to pay their rent for the first three months but they were told that they would be on their own after that.

By their third day in Montreal, Erna and Horst were at an employment agency looking for work. Horst was sent to a company that was looking for people to work at shippers. He had no idea what that was but it paid $18 for a six-day workweek, so the next day he went to the address given to him. He had no idea what he signed on for when he took the job.

It turned out to be a garment distribution center and his job consisted of putting garments into a box, sealing it, and affixing a pre-addressed sticker on it for shipment. Bored, he quit after only a week to find something more challenging. He returned to the employment office where he was told that they had just the right job for him.

He was sent to Martin's Swiss Repair Shop, where he was interviewed carefully and then hired on the spot. It was owned and operated by two men in their early fifties. They were French-Canadian, bilingual, and nice guys to work for, Horst was pleased to discover. The business sold and repaired bikes and tricycles, baby carriages, and many other items. In addition, Roul Oligny, one of the partners, was a master locksmith who also repaired radios, the type with tubes, resistors, condensers, and a great deal of wiring. He shared his knowledge with Horst and taught him how to sharpen knives, scissors, and mower blades, as well as how to weld.

The other partner, Tony, was the outside man, also a locksmith but he had many other trades too. Horst found this a laidback business to work for and a great place for him to learn. They paid him $35 per week, almost double that of the first job, and worked for five and a half days every week.

The front of the shop was reserved for bicycles, baby carriages, and an assortment of other related merchandise. The back served as the repair shop, which eventually became Horst's domain. He loved working there, there was never a dull moment and there was always something different to work on.

With Roul's help, Horst learned to speak English. Despite his best efforts to teach Horst proper sentence structure and pronunciation, there are still many words that he mispronounces today. He claims that's how people know he is from another country. To further his English skills, Horst began reading books, pocket-sized to make it easier for him to carry them with him. He started with Westerns, they were easy to read, the plots easy to follow, and the good guys always came out on top. While reading, he started to copy the text word for word and that helped him with his spelling. It was a slow process, but one that worked.

Erna had a more difficult time fitting in. She looked for work in the garment industry as a machine operator. The first job she landed lasted all of four hours before she was politely told to get some experience first and return when she felt she could handle the job. She kept trying, each job she got lasted a little longer than the one before and she learned a little more with each one. In most places she worked, kind women showed her what to do and how to do it. Before long, Erna could handle the work on her own. Horst always admired her tenacity.

One day, after having been let go from two different jobs in the same morning, Erna was too embarrassed to return home so she went to a movie house that was open 24 hours a day and played a feature film, along with a newsreel, and a cartoon. She stayed there a while and went home later than usual, she told Selma that she had put in some overtime. Finding and keeping jobs wasn't easy for her but she always worked. She was extremely proud and independent. She worked and supported herself and her mother when it counted most.

The three Sterns were finally becoming self-sufficient. Horst and Erna were making enough money to stand on their own two feet and they declined any more handouts from the HIAS. It was 1952 and Horst suddenly realized that they had been "on the dole" since 1946. It was about time for them to become independent and take charge of their own lives. Although, they were grateful for the assistance given to them when they needed it the most, getting up each morning and going to work to receive a paycheck at the end of the week was good for one's self-esteem.

Time went by, they went to the movies at least once a week with his grandmother sitting next to Erna asking her constantly, "What did he say?" And they saved enough money to buy her German language newspapers. Life continued until one day Horst received a phone call at work.

Selma's landlady called Horst and told him to come home right away because his grandmother had fallen and injured herself. By the time Horst reached the house, he noticed that an ambulance was already there. Erna was already in the ambulance and after Horst identified himself, he was able join them on the ride to the hospital.

After arriving at the hospital, Selma was removed from the ambulance and Horst and Erna were told to go to the waiting room, and so the waiting game began. Hour after hour crept by and every time they asked about his grandmother, they received the same reply; they were running some tests. Finally, someone approached them with the verdict. As a result of the fall, Selma had broken a hip and they were given a room number so they could go see her.

Horst and his mother entered the room and there she was, his grandmother, all four foot eight of her, lying in the bed. She appeared almost lost in it and she wore an apologetic look on her face, as if it were her fault. There wasn't much Horst and Erna could do for her. They brought her some German newspapers which they knew would make her happy and they left her with the promise to return the following day. Arriving home to where Erna lived, they suddenly realized how empty a house could be when one of its members wasn't there.

It took about two weeks for the hospital to release Selma but once she was home it seemed as if everything would pick up where it left off. The only difference was that she had to be very careful whenever she moved. Soon after her return though, they received a phone call from the doctor who had taken care of her in the hospital. He requested to speak with them about Selma's condition. They made the appointment immediately.

Once they were with the doctor, he explained that while Selma had been in the hospital he had run a few tests and with the results in, they discovered that she had cancer and that there was nothing they could do for her. He said the most they could hope for was that she might have another six months to live. The doctor then gave Horst some ampoules of morphine and showed him how to administer it to his grandmother. He remembers he had to pull the plastic top off the syringe to expose the needle, break the top off of the ampoule with his thumb and forefinger, dip the needle in and extract the morphine and then insert it into her thigh. The morphine was automatically released and acted almost immediately.

The only consolation was that Selma didn't suffer for long. With the amount of morphine Horst and Erna had at their disposal, they were able to spare her unnecessary pain. Sometimes days or a week went by when she didn't feel any pain. That's when they thought that everything would be all right after all. But time took its toll and she got worse. Horst helped control her pain as much as he could but Selma was 87 years old. He remembers,

"Even though she had the heart of a lioness, it finally gave out. She died in my arms... My grandmother was a woman who never complained." (Stern, 2006)

When the family lived in Berlin, before the war, she was the matriarch of the family. She was one of seven children, five girls and two boys. She wasn't the oldest but the one with the most fire within. Anytime there was a dispute amongst the sisters they would say, "Let's ask Selma she will know what to do."

Selma and Horst would talk frequently and she would say that she felt sorry for the two of them, he and Erna, because she was being such a burden and as far she was concerned she was ready to go. All Horst could say was, "Never mind that; when your time is up we will let you know. Meanwhile, we have plenty of time left."

He says now, "I really loved that woman. She was the first person I loved totally to the end and beyond. Till I die." There were a few others he loved in between that turned out to be more of the physical kind of love until one day, in the 70s, he finally met the woman who would become his wife, Barbara. He explains theirs as the type of love that grows over time, they have been together for 40 plus years, and he wouldn't know what to do without her, but he says, "Don't tell her I said that."

It was a sad day when Horst and Erna buried Selma in the Jewish Cemetery in Montreal. It rained that day so he felt even the skies were crying at her passing. She lived to be 87 years old and although her life wasn't an easy one, she persevered and she was one of the very few of their extensive family that the Nazis didn't get a hold. She died in her own bed, a luxury not afforded to many and her grandson would always take pride and comfort in knowing that.

After the passing of Selma, life wasn't the same for the remaining Sterns. Their small family had been a very close unit. Not long after the three of them had arrived in Montreal, Selma's cousin Irma and her husband had come to visit them. They hadn't seen each other since 1923, her cousin had left Germany with her family for Israel, returned, and then left again for Paris, where they were fortunate enough to get visas for America. She had emigrated there with her husband and two children.

Cousin Irma and her husband stayed with the Sterns for a couple of days and even offered to take Selma back with them to New York. There, they had a big house with plenty of room and they could give Selma much more than Erna and Horst could. Erna told cousin Irma that she would call her in a few days to let her know what Selma decided about the kind and heart-felt offer. When they were alone again and asked Selma what she thought about the opportunity, all she said was, "Oh no. You won't get rid of me that easily."

Erna called New York and gave Irma the bad news about her mother's passing. Irma asked if there was anything that she could do for them and that's when Erna said that she would like to go to live in America. Her cousin said that she would see what she could do about getting her a visa. True to her word, not long after Selma's death, a visa arrived for Erna to fulfill her dream of emigrating to America.

Horst on the other hand wasn't too keen on the idea of going to the United States. It was 1952, the war in Korea was in full swing and he had had his fill of wars. After surviving two, he didn't want to push his luck. He was certain that if he had gone to the United Stated with Erna, he would have been enlisted. He says his personal history could have been altered and posted to a sign that would read something like, "Here he lies, almost made it, but it wasn't to be." It was a chance he wasn't willing to take.

However, Horst didn't stay in Montreal long after his mother left. He knew he needed a change of scenery. He remembered that one of his cousins told him about a sister-in-law of his in Toronto. He had told her about Horst and they extended an invitation for him to come meet them. He hated to leave his job but Montreal just wasn't the same without his mother and grandmother, so he explained his situation to his employers, they understood and wished him luck on his new endeavors. Other than that, he didn't really have anyone else to say good bye to. He packed the one and only suitcase that he owned, went to the train station and bought a one-way ticket to Toronto.

The ride was uneventful. He arrived early in the morning and had to wait about half an hour before the diner opened for breakfast. He finally ordered something to eat and by the time he had finished more people were arriving, so he asked some people if they knew of a local boarding house. They recommended using a phone book and he wondered why he hadn't thought of that himself. One man helped him narrow down his search and he managed to find an address.

Next, Horst bought a map of the city and looked up the address of the boarding house, and that of his cousin's sister-in-law. The two addresses weren't too far from one another. Taking the subway, Horst soon found the boarding house. He spoke with the woman who owned it and after looking around he found the room clean and spacious so he asked the price. He found it to be quite reasonable, considering it included three meals a day, breakfast, packed lunch, and a regular meal in the evening. He asked if he could move in that day. She said if he paid for the first week, he could consider himself moved in.

He wouldn't have the room to himself though. While unpacking his few belongings, he met his new roommate. He was about Horst's age and as they started talking, he found out that he was from Finland and had immigrated to Canada not long before.

Horst's next stop was the state employment office. Thanks to his street map, he found it without a problem. Once there, he was given a form to fill out on which he had to list whatever work experience he had. He put down that he had worked as a bicycle mechanic in Montreal for the last two years and returned the paper. In less than five minutes, the employment office gave him a document with an address to go to. He found the shop, the job and shop were very similar to what he had left in Montreal. They also focused on bicycles and repairs, only instead of baby carriages, they sold skis, ski equipment, and skates. He had found himself a new home in Toronto.

24

TORONTO

Horst, already adept at bicycle repair, enjoyed learning new skills and trades such as how to sharpen ice skate blades on a special machine. In addition to this, the shop owner taught him how to bind and route skis. As the only so-called mechanic working there, the variety of repairs that he was asked to perform were vast. It was a constant learning process.

During his second week in Toronto, Horst finally reached out to his cousin's sister-in-law. Once he identified himself, she told him that she had been expecting his call and they made arrangements for him to go to their home that Saturday for lunch.

They became fast friends, lunch soon turned to dinner and finally Horst accepted their invitation to spend the night. As he eventually headed back to his own place after having spent most of the next day there as well, he felt fortunate to have met such fine new friends. He remained in touch with them throughout his life.

Toronto was a fairly dull town in 1954. To a young man like Horst, it seemed that come Friday afternoon, the town elders pulled the sidewalks in and reinstalled them on Monday mornings so people could go back to work. He assumed the churches made out all right because there was nothing much else to do.

Boredom set in quickly. Horst had some Canadian friends from his boarding house who he felt were afflicted with the same disease he had, wanderlust. He doesn't remember where the idea came from but he thought owning a car might help alleviate the situation for all of them.

The prospect of owning a vehicle was both exhilarating and frightening. The idea that he would owe money to a bank, or anyone else for that matter, was foreign to him. He was raised to save for whatever he wanted to purchase and buy it once he could afford to without financial assistance for any of it. Stepping out of his comfort zone, he approached a second-hand car lot.

Once the seasoned salesman got hold of Horst, there was little hope of backing out. He assured Horst that if anything went wrong with the vehicle in the first a week, Horst could return it for a full refund. Reluctantly, he handed over the down payment of $100 for a 1947 four-door Chevy sedan and drove away. At 26 years old, he had just bought his first car.

In addition to the down payment, Horst agreed to pay $50, plus interest, per month for the next six months at which time a total of $400 would be paid and the car would be his. It seemed like a fortune to him and the burden weighed heavily upon him. The first night after his new purchase, he hardly slept a wink.

"The idea that I owed anyone such a sum of money bothered the hell out of me. The car rode well, and there was nothing I could see wrong, and I couldn't find a reason to return the car to the dealer. I had a panic attack, plain and simple. I saw losing my job and not being able to make my monthly payment. I got so paranoid that I actually drove back to the place and almost begged the salesman to take the car back, that I even would forfeit the down payment of the $100." (Stern, 2006)

The salesman refused to take the car back. He just informed Horst, "Mister, you bought the car; you pay for it. If you fall behind with your payments, we repossess the car and sell it again. Meanwhile, have fun driving it."

When he reflects on that incident, he still wonders why they didn't take him up on his offer. It would have been a win-win situation for them. He thinks perhaps they didn't understand him and assumed he had some sort of ulterior motive. Regardless of the reasons, it appeared that Horst had actually found an honest used car dealer. It turned out to be a reliable vehicle that served him well and he paid it off in record time. Even to this day he is uncomfortable with credit. He will use a credit card but pays it off in full, whenever possible, when he receives the bill.

With a car to accommodate their thirst for adventure, Horst and the two Canadian men he met at the boarding house set out on an adventure. The three of them decided to head to Vancouver, sharing the cost of gas and repairs along the way. They set a departure date and Horst quit his job and said his good byes to his friends.

The group decided to make a detour to New York first, mainly because Erna was living there with the rest of the family and one of the other guys had an aunt living there who he hadn't seen for some time. Partner number three had never seen New York and was eager to spend a couple of days there. Horst enjoyed seeing the whole family again.

Erna had found a small apartment near her cousin's house in Brooklyn. She had found a job in Manhattan as a sewing machine operator in the garment center and was relatively happy.

After a couple of days, Horst said good bye to his family and the three young men piled into his car and began, what they believed was a 3,000-mile trip. It was summer and they had brought their sleeping bags with them. The weather cooperated most of the time. The few times it rained, they just kept driving, taking turns to stretch out on back seat and rest.

Once they taught partner number three to drive, they switched drivers every three or four hours, thus making good time. They would pull over onto the grass next to the road at night. After eating cold food out of cans, they would crawl into their sleeping bags and get some rest. In the morning, they got back on the road to find a diner where they could freshen up and order a hardy breakfast. From there, after a few flat tires and an engine issue, they eventually reached their destination of Vancouver.

Vancouver was an amazing city with mountains on one side and the Pacific Ocean on the other. They found a boarding house and moved in. Since his car had been acting up and he didn't really need one any more, he went to a used car dealer and sold it. After some haggling, they agreed to $150.

Upon returning to the boarding house, Horst learned that one of his travel companions had taken a job with a gas company as an office worker. The other man and Horst both decided to visit an employment agency on the waterfront. As expected, there was a fee for their services. At the busy office, Horst's friend was called in first for an interview. He came out grinning and waving to him and Horst knew, at once, that he had landed a job. He approached Horst, they said their goodbyes there as he had to leave for the job right away. That was the last time the two ever saw each other.

Shortly after, Horst was called into the office and the man asked if he had worked, in any capacity, at a lumber camp. Horst replied that he was an extremely fast learner and was willing to take any job they might offer. The interviewer smiled and said, "All right young man. From now on, call yourself a whistle punk." With that done, he was asked his name, age, and next of kin. Then he gave Horst his fee. He dug into his pocket and paid him the requested sum.

Horst was told to be at the airport the next morning and was reminded to make sure he had enough money to pay for the flight. Although excited for his new adventure, there was just one question nagging him. *What on earth is a whistle punk?* He realized that he probably wouldn't discover the answer until he reached his destination and hoped that someone would be kind enough to explain it to him when he got there.

The small charter plane, that accommodated Horst and four other lumber camp-bound men, provided an incredibly beautiful one-hour flight. Flying above and between the Rocky Mountains was an experience that he has never forgotten. The plane had pontoons, allowing them to land on a lake. The pilot taxied the plane to the dock and they exited right into the lumber camp where Horst would spend the next six months.

The camp consisted of a dirt main street with about six bunkhouses on each side. One of them served as an office where

Horst presented the piece of paper he received from the agent in Vancouver. After receiving his bunk assignment, he entered the house and saw four beds. Three of them were occupied, so he took the only one remaining. He stored his meager belongings in the locker next to it.

While walking down the road, he came across a store that sold all of the equipment needed for being a logger. He opted for steel tipped boots with hobnails for better traction for walking up and down the logs. He was told to stick to long sleeved flannel shirts, of which he bought two, plus heavy socks, a thermos, and other necessities. He didn't have to pay for any of it up front and was told that it would be deducted from his first paycheck.

He roamed around the camp and found the most important building, the mess hall. There was a pool room and better yet, a room full of books, mostly Westerns and crime stories. He loved Westerns and still does once in a while, especially those by Louis L'amour. Henry says, "Reading those stories, at least you know where you stand. The bad guys always lose."

Horst returned to his bunkhouse and met his bunkmates. They asked him if he played poker. He explained that he didn't gamble because he tried putting some money on a horse race once and that sucker was still trying to find the finish line. They never asked him about it again. He watched in amazement as they lost an entire month's pay on the turn of a card.

The food in camp was phenomenal. Steak and eggs were available for anyone who wanted them, juice, pancakes, and so on, it was a far cry from the years of starvation he had endured. The workers were provided with the fixings to make and pack their own lunches before they went off to work. The food was plentiful but alcohol was absolutely not permitted.

Getting to work consisted of hopping onto a truck that took them about five miles down a dirt road. They would get off the truck and head up the mountain to a spot where another crew had felled all the trees on a particular slope. Once all of the branches were cleared off the logs, Horst's crew came in and transported the felled trees down the slope to the road, where a machine lifted them onto trucks that drove them to a spot where the logs were sluiced down to the lake. From there, another crew took them to the mills.

One day, Horst heard that the guy who worked in the kitchen had quit and that they were looking for a replacement. That was all he needed to hear. He went to the office and told them that he had some kitchen experience and convinced them to give him a chance to prove he could do the job. The man in charge agreed and from them on, he worked in the kitchen. He realized that he wasn't lumberjack material. He had tried it for three months and it was an interesting experience but he learned that he would rather see the trees grow than help chop them down.

Horst and the chef got along fine. His experience in the army helped him a lot. He did what he was told to while the chef consumed any ingredients that had traces of alcohol in them. Vanilla extract, shaving lotion, and who knows what else. He was a functioning alcoholic but he was an excellent chef. In the time Horst was there, "nobody died or got food poisoning." Considering that he was drunk most of the time that was quite an accomplishment.

Horst stuck it out at the logging camp for the season and when the camp closed for the winter he returned to Vancouver and was lucky enough to find lodging at the same place as before.

In all the time he was up in the lumber camp, he spent very little money. Only buying the necessities, like toothpaste, soap, and cigarettes, resulted in him saving quite a bundle of money. Horst had stayed in touch with his mother, who told him that she was working on a visa for him to immigrate. He sent Erna $500, just for the fun of it, and learned that she used it to get a nose job.

Using the most inexpensive means of travel available at the time, Horst took a bus from Vancouver to New York. The ride was enjoyable, but it took five days. When the journey ended, he took the BMT (now called the subway) to the Brighton Beach Station and walked to the address Erna had given him in her last letter.

Erna rented a two bedroom, three-story, walkup on 13th Street. Once there, he rang the bell and was reunited with his mother.

They paused to reflect on the fact that they had finally made it. Their odyssey had started in Budapest in early 1946, with a few detours and six years later, they reached the goal they had set for themselves. It wasn't a total victory, they lost their main player, Selma.

The apartment was only two blocks from the beach. Coney Island was just two subway stops away, which was great for the weekends but he needed to get to work during the week. At 27 years old, he had worked many jobs but what he knew best was working with bicycles, so he wisely looked for a job in that field. Three days after he arrived, he secured a job at a bicycle shop on Coney Island Avenue. He worked five and a half days a week for $65.

This was the first time in Horst's life, not including Berlin when he was younger, that he lived with family. He spent a lot of time with several cousins. It was customary for the whole family to meet at his aunt and uncle's house on Sundays and holidays for family dinner. He reflects fondly on those times and remembers how good it felt to always be included.

After working in the bicycle shop for about six months, Horst realized that he was on the wrong path. He received a raise but the job got boring. His cousin's wife suggested that he could try becoming a waiter. He would get to meet a lot of new people while making good money. He took the chance, realizing that if it didn't work out for him, he could always return to bike repair.

With the assistance of the Manhattan telephone book, Horst was able to find many listings for agencies that specialized in placing people in temporary positions such as maids, waiters, and hotel staff in Manhattan, Long Island, and the Catskill Mountains. After locating the large building and going through the interview process, he was assigned to a job in a small town called Tarrytown in New York. Fortunately, he had purchased a used car, which was definitely needed for the new position.

Horst's jaw dropped as he reached the address on his assignment card. As he entered the open gate and followed the long driveway, he came upon a grand chateau that turned out to be a very exclusive country club. As it turned out, this job was quite easy.

It was off-season so most of the club members were gone. That ended up being a good thing as he had a lot to learn. Thankfully, the chef and bartender helped him as much as they could.

The job consisted of serving three meals a day and the most he had to serve at one seating was perhaps three or four couples. The downside of off-season was that the potential to make good money wasn't there. However, he got free room and board and found the overall experience priceless. The place dripped with atmosphere and old money. He was told that some of the Rockefellers were members there.

Within a month though, he and everyone else working there was laid off and the kitchen and dining room closed, indefinitely. He returned to the employment agency and was sent to a seafood house in Stamford-Darian in Connecticut. Again he had to learn, this time it involved learning one fish from another. It was too far from Brooklyn so he rented a room in the neighborhood. He had a roommate but he only stayed there long enough to sleep so it didn't matter to him. On his one day off, he would go to Brooklyn to see his family. He kept this job and routine for about six months before heading back to Brooklyn to live and begin a new assignment on Long Island. At last, in 1956, he started making good money.

Wanderlust struck once again as the cold New York winter set in and Horst was off again. This time, he headed to South Florida. After 23 hours on the road, he arrived in Miami, found a room off Collins Avenue and had a good sleep. After a hearty breakfast the next morning, he went from restaurant to restaurant looking for a job and at last found one at The Fontainebleau Hotel. He describes it as "uppity and beautiful," but there were more waiters than customers. At least he saw some famous people like the Marx brothers and Vic Damon.

After three weeks, he quit and got "a real waiter's job." Horst worked for a Jewish delicatessen that sat about 40 people. He said the menu was about a half a mile long but fortunately the items were numbered, which made ordering easier. He says it was like an organized madhouse.

Once again, after four months, he quit and headed back to

Brooklyn but this time he didn't take a steady job. Instead, he worked a lot as an extra waiter on weekends, sometimes traveling to the Catskills for work before settling in, such as it was, to a steady job again.

Soon, Horst's family, in the Brooklyn area, showed interest in purchasing a hotel. They decided to put a coffee shop in and asked Horst and one of his cousins to run it. He opened the shop in the mornings and worked through lunchtime and his cousin came in during the afternoon and worked until closing time. They both shared the food prep and they made a pretty good team. Once a week, he went to the farmers market and bought whatever they needed for the week. It was a challenge but he loved every minute of it.

They were in business for about a year when the bosses decided the place needed some renovations, a bigger grill and a better coffee machine, among other things. They decided to close the place down for about ten days for the renovations. During this time, Horst's cousin Leo, the one who Horst ran the coffee shop with, came up with the idea of going to the Virgin Islands. Someone in the family had gone to St. Thomas and raved about its beauty, the fabulous beaches, and clear water. Horst readily accepted Leo's invitation.

Leo's wife, Dorothy, joined them on the trip, as well as their two daughters, aged ten and five. He isn't sure whether they adopted him or he them but he spent more time at their home than with his mother since he had come to the United States. They made reservations for one week and flew to their destination. Once he settled into his room, he made the mistake of drinking the water, which left him violently ill for the first three days of the trip.

Once Horst trusted that he could venture out, he was most impressed with the island's beauty. He was especially drawn to Magens Beach, which at that time was almost untouched by man. The water was transparent all the way down to 100 feet. There were no hotels or condominiums. All of that came later. They all truly enjoyed their vacation but it came to an end too soon and they had to pack for their return trip to New York.

Upon their return, they discovered the renovations had been completed as promised. Horst received a new grill with double the capacity he had before, a new gas stove with an oven and six burners, and a bigger coffee brewing machine, all of which was intended to make his life easier. His cousin, Rita, painted a mural on one of the walls. The place looked great. Yet, Horst still wasn't happy or content. He found he couldn't get the islands that he had just visited out of his mind.

Horst went to the local library and researched the islands and with the knowledge he gained, he set his mind on moving to St. Croix. Meanwhile, the coffee shop was doing fine but his heart just wasn't in it any more. He no longer saw running a coffee shop and waiting tables as a career. A change was long overdue. He decided to look for a plumber's helper position.

Horst found the position that he was looking for and was hired right away. Taking a salary cut to begin with, he figured he would eventually make the money back once he was skilled enough. The plumbing shop for which he worked was in Brooklyn. At first, he simply handed the skilled plumbers the tools or fittings they requested but before long, he was able to handle small repairs and was sent to do many repair jobs in apartment buildings. He read many plumbing books from the library and it opened up a whole new world for him. Within six months of training on the job, he quit. With the tools of the trade that he had been purchasing with his paychecks, he decided to pursue his dream and start his own plumbing business on St. Croix.

25

ST. CROIX

By this time, Horst had been in the United States for five years and he was finally eligible for American citizenship. On April 25, 1961, he not only became an American citizen but also legally changed his name to Henry. He believes that his life changed for the better from that day on.

When the time came for Horst, now Henry, to pack for his journey to St. Croix in the Virgin Islands, he realized just how many tools he had actually purchased. He needed a steamer trunk and several pieces of luggage for all of his possessions, he boarded the ship in New Jersey which was the least expensive way to get himself and everything he owned to his destination. He was pleasantly surprised to find that his outside cabin, with a bathroom of its own and intended for four people, would be all his. There were actually only 12 other passengers on the entire ship. For the 11-day trip, they dined in the officers' mess hall, drank a lot, and played cards or read.

At the stops in San Juan, Puerto Rico, Mayaguez, and Ponce, there was plenty of time for the passengers to disembark and see each town. St. Thomas was the final destination for the majority of the passengers. By the time they reached St. Croix, only Henry and two ladies remained onboard. Before long, he was standing on the dock in the town of Fredericksted surrounded by a large pile of luggage. Suddenly, overwhelmed by the giant leap he had just taken, he let out a silent yell, *Henry, you schmuck, what the hell are you doing here?* He couldn't have known that as he stood there, this would be his home, on and off, for the next 25 years.

That wasn't the first time Henry stood on a new shore, alone, not knowing anyone at all but he had made it before and he knew he would make it this time too. The one thing he had in his favor was that at least this time, he spoke the language.

So, there he stood without anyone to greet him but then he hadn't expected anyone. As he stood on the pier, he noticed a man standing next to a panel truck looking at him, so Henry walked over and asked the man for help. The man asked him where he wanted to go and Henry explained that he had booked a hotel room at the Pink Fancy in Christiansted. The man replied, "Shore, Mon," and they loaded his luggage into the truck. The ride took about 45 minutes and was filled with early, unspoiled views of donkey carts and lush vegetation.

Henry talked to the driver about how and why he had come to the island and explained that he wanted to get away from the city and enjoy life. The man confirmed that Henry had chosen the right place and as they arrived at the hotel and unloaded the truck, Henry asked how much he owed him for his trouble. To Henry's surprise, the man's response was, "No charge. Welcome to St. Croix. I hope you make it here." At a loss for words, Henry tried to put some money in the man's hand but he just shook his head. Henry thanked him profusely as he drove off and had a good feeling that this was a great start.

Henry saw the man several times over the years he invited him out for drinks a few times. As they got to know each other better, he learned the man had come to St. Croix from Puerto Rico, with his parents, many years earlier and that Henry would find many others like him on the island. The native population were friendly and helpful.

After settling in the hotel and taking a little time to enjoy the swimming pool, Henry walked to a restaurant for a meal. On the way, he noticed a large construction site. He made a mental note to return to it the next day. Following a swim and breakfast the next morning, he walked to the site, which turned out to be a low-cost housing project. He spoke to the supervisor and was referred to the man in charge of plumbing. The man asked Henry about his experience and once he heard that Henry had been a plumber's assistant he offered Henry 75 cents per hour. Henry thanked him but moved on. Henry went to the Virgin Island Employment Agency next, where he looked for work as a cook. He was offered a job at the local penitentiary. He would be required to work six days a week for $35. He politely declined.

On day three, Henry met up with the two ladies who had also been on the ship coming to St. Croix. They both loved The Grape Tree Bay Hotel, where they both were staying, and once they discovered that Henry wasn't working yet, they offered to ask their hotel manager if he had a job available for him.

He was somewhat discouraged when he thought about his rent that was due in four days but he reminded himself that he had survived two wars and he would survive this too. He had enough money with him to last six months but he would feel better if he had a steady paycheck. By the fifth day, he had a message at the office from The Grape Tree Bay Hotel. They wanted him to go in for an interview, at which he was hired immediately.

Henry's new job, as an assistant salad chef, came with free room and board. The lodging consisted of a room in a barrack-like building divided into a dozen rooms where the staff were housed. Henry shared a room with another man. He worked six days a week but had enough time off during the day to go snorkeling or swimming. He only lasted about three weeks in the position though.

One day, Henry was called into the office. The manager asked him if he would be interested in working the front desk, effective immediately. The woman who normally worked at reception had an emergency back home in the States and had to leave immediately. The new position came with a few perks. He would have to move into one of the bungalows, which just happened to overlook the Caribbean Sea. He would also receive a higher salary and dine in the guest dining room, there was a table set aside for the employees. The use of the pool was also encouraged. Henry naturally jumped at the offer. He felt he had died and gone to Heaven. The job only lasted about six months as the hotel's contract with a large air conditioning company ended. All the extra staff that were hired were no longer needed once all the company's representatives vacated the premises. Henry considers his time there as the longest paid vacation he had ever had.

Homeless once again, Henry found a large two-bedroom apartment in the middle of town. It had a kitchen, living room, and was on the ground floor of a private house. He soon took in one of his former coworkers from the hotel to share expenses. He found small plumbing jobs to pay for his own share.

At 34 years old, Henry drifted aimlessly through life, working only to exist. He knew what was missing in his life, the lack of a philosophy to live by. He had long since given up on religion of any kind but he was left with the nagging question of how and why everything came about. He admits at that time he was still under the impression there was a higher power, a nameless creator. He would later dig deeper into this to try find some answers.

A neighbor helped Henry get a job as a house painter. His first painting job was quite memorable, it was a big three-story house that was purchased by Victor Borge, a famous pianist and comedian. The inside had been gutted and was renovated inside and out and everything needed to be painted. Henry got to meet Mr. Borge and spoke with him on a few occasions. He refers to him as a "nice man and talented snowbird." Halfway through the job, Mr. Borge decided he didn't like the color originally selected and chose a different one.

Henry claims he took to a paintbrush like a duck to water. The life of a painter was a good fit for him. He was able to work on one project for a short period of time and then move on for a change of scenery, leaving him little time to get bored. He felt he had finally found a job he could turn into his trade and career.

Henry's boss, Bill, got ambitious and expanded the business. He started to accept painting jobs in St. Thomas and had enough work to keep six painters busy for a while. However, instead of hiring them on St. Thomas, he decided to buy a small houseboat made out of 50-gallon oil drums with a deck bolted on top of them. The framework consisted of two-by-fours with cutouts for the window shutters, that could be raised for ventilation, and a few partitions to give the illusion that is was a three-bedroom home. There was also an outhouse.

The roof was made of corrugated metal siding and there was a stove for cooking. A home away from home. For fresh water, they used five-gallon cans they had to ferry over in a dingy they used to get to and from shore to their make-shift houseboat. There were six workers living on the boat and they had to make sure that nobody got stuck on shore overnight so they came up with a curfew. If someone wasn't back by 11 p.m., they either swam or spent the night with a girl, if they had one. Henry loved every minute of it. He remembers, "After all, I was 34 years old going on 16 years old, just a kid."

After having moved onto the houseboat, they started work on a new hotel. Everything went well for a couple of weeks but then Bill ran into trouble with the harbormaster.

It was 1962 and many others had the same idea to try avoid high rents. They built themselves make-shift lodgings by putting up shacks on pontoons and lived as cheaply as possible in paradise. By the time they had made their place livable, there must have been at least another 50 of those so-called houseboats anchored in the harbor which didn't sit too well with the legitimate boat owners and yacht people who anchored there.

"The open toilets of those 50-odd houseboats produced enough stinky material to choke a horse, if the breeze was right. So, with a stroke of the pen, the elders passed a law so we became instant outlaws and given something like 48 hours to install holding tanks for the effluent produced by those living on the houseboat, and those who would not abide to this edict would be fined rather heavily, and their houseboats impounded.

Most of the owners of those houseboats just cleaned out everything that was of any value, and disappeared, never to be seen or heard from again. You had a few die-hards, but they did not last very long, and Pontoon City, as some of the people had started to call it, was no more.

I assume that a government crew was sent out to clean up that ugly mess. Needless to say, this was the end of our stay in St. Thomas, and back to St. Croix it was." (Stern, 2006)

Following a few other painting jobs with Bill and some financial issues in which he was owed pay, he became disenchanted with the island and wanderlust struck again. Soon Henry forgot the beauty that surrounded him and he suddenly couldn't wait to "get off that rock in the middle of the Caribbean Sea." He still hadn't found his identity and was forever searching for something but he didn't know what it was. He had no idea what motivated him but in 1963, he decided to return to New York to try figure it out.

Fortunately, Erna had kept the apartment in Brooklyn and Henry was able to move back into his old room. With some of the money he had from selling most of his tools before moving back to the States, he offered to take his mother on a trip to Berlin to see her sister. Erna hadn't seen her since 1949.

The two of them flew to Berlin with a stopover in Amsterdam, Henry found to be a very interesting city. For the three days they were there, they visited the Anne Frank House and other landmarks. They had planned to go on to Copenhagen but Erna got sick and had to fly directly to Berlin. Erna stayed with her sister and her husband but because of lack of space, Henry stayed at one of the nearby guesthouses.

While in Berlin, Henry and Erna put in a requisition for some kind of reparation from the German government for the hell they had been put through from the day Hitler came to power in 1933 through to the end of the war. Despite working in the office of reparation (for Holocaust survivors) in Munich after she left Israel, Erna never thought to apply for her own compensation. After finding the right office and the right official to talk to, Erna shared their story. She told them they escaped to Hungary from Germany before being captured by the Nazis in 1940. The official told them that if the Nazis had captured them up and sent them to a concentration camp, they would have a case to present to the proper officials who handled them but because they left the country voluntarily, there was nothing he could do for them. That kind of logic was hard to digest but it was all that was offered to them in the 1963.

Since then, Henry has met numerous Jewish refugees from Germany, Austria, and other eastern European countries who succeeded in escaping into Hungary during the war. They were later rounded up by the Hungarian Nazis and put into cattle cars and shipped to Russia where they ended up in slave labor battalions. "There were few survivors, but I am sure that Germany didn't take responsibility for their deaths either; after all they did leave their country voluntarily." The injustice of all of it still haunts him to this day.

After returning to New York, Henry once again found work as a painter. However, light work in the winter had him, once again, taking inventory of life. He was 36 years old and still shared an apartment with his mother. His funds were limited as was his security about being out on his own. Up until then, he had worked many jobs but still felt that he was a master of none.

Henry began dreaming of the island again but knew he needed to save up money again to make it work. The fastest way to get it was to go back to waiting tables so he reinstated with the Waiter's Union. He was sent to his first assignment at Manero's Steak House on Syosset in Long Island. It turned out to be a nice place to work. They didn't serve breakfast, just lunch and dinner. It involved long hours but the money was good.

Even though he loved the little '57 Volkswagen Beetle he purchased from an acquaintance, the drive from Brooklyn to Long Island once again became too much for him so he rented a room closer to work. On his days off, he drove home to be with family. During this time he had a friend named Jack who was quite intelligent. Following conversations about books they had each read, Jack asked Henry if he was familiar with Ayn Rand. Henry began with her novelette, *We the Living*, and then progressed to *The Fountainhead* and *Atlas Shrugged*. The latter, he says, "Really blew my mind." While reading those books, he came to the realization that he had found a worthwhile philosophy and decided to research it in more depth.

The more he learned about this new philosophy, the more he wanted to know. He started to realize how deeply he was tuned in to something that resembled his own value system. That was the first time he saw it in black and white with an explanation attached to it. This philosophy, called objectivism, dealt with the facts of life for what they were, regardless of the perceiver. According to Henry, "Objectivism is best verbalized by Ayn Rand, 'My philosophy, in essence is the concept of a man as a heroic being, with his own happiness as the moral purpose of his life, with productive achievement as his noblest activity, and reason as his only absolute.'"

Henry attended some of her discussion groups where the subject was the role of philosophy, the government and the individual, logic and mysticism, the nature of love, and many other topics. It was the first time in his life that he had met someone who was able verbalize the content of a philosophy into plain English so that a lay person, such as himself, could understand. Previously, he had felt that most philosophies were ruled by blind feelings or strict obedience with the penalty of eternal damnation. He was astonished by how much his life changed with his new-found understanding of the identification of reality. It didn't happen overnight and he intends to continue studying it until the day he dies but the knowledge that reality will prevail until the end of time is satisfying to know.

Finally, Henry realized that he had saved enough money to move on, so he quit his job, bought an additional vehicle, shipped his belongings ahead, and left for St. Croix and returned to the Pink Fancy Hotel. There, he planned to stay on a day-to-day basis while he looked for his own place. By the second day, he met someone who gave him a lead for an efficiency apartment that required no lease and provided him a home on a month-to-month basis. He picked up one of his vehicles, a Volkswagen bus, which was full of tools that he had shipped over. He had been warned not to load anything into it because Customs would confiscate anything they deemed not necessary to drive the vehicle, but fortunately, nothing seemed to be disturbed. He made arrangements to pick up his car the next day and he left to begin his new life.

Henry visited the people he had known there before to reestablish some connections, one of which paid off immediately. At the plumbing supply store, the owner complained that he had been broken into several times. It was a large store with an efficiency apartment attached. He offered it to Henry so that he could stay there each night and act as security for him. He rented it to him for $20 a month instead than listing him as an employee on the books. The deal worked out well for both of them. Henry moved in immediately, and the arrangement lasted for a year after which the owner moved his business to a new location.

While Henry lived at the store, he found some plumbing work but was soon informed that he needed a license to be a plumber. He studied for it and took the necessary exam and received his Master Plumber Certificate. Between plumbing and the occasional paint job, he was able to make a living.

One day while having coffee at a local restaurant, Henry ran into his former boss, Bill, who still owed him $600 but who also taught him how to paint. After they discussed where each of their lives had recently led, they talked about creating a partnership. Bill's credit was shot on the island at that time so everything had to be in Henry's name, but together they started their painting company. Bill did the bidding and secured the jobs. Henry did the financing and ran the jobsite. Bill also put in time on the job when time permitted. Soon they had big jobs and an eight-man crew. Bill and Henry took only token salaries to build up a cash reserve and Bill kept the books. Henry saw no reason not to trust him until the day Bill told him they didn't have enough money in the reserve to pay for some of the materials they had used.

After confronting him, the only excuse Bill could offer was that he couldn't live on the agreed salary and he had more mouths to feed so had taken a bigger salary. He told Henry not to worry because he kept track of the difference and of what the business owed Henry. Some quick decisions had to be made about whether to close the company or try come up with some fast money to try stay in business. He decided to call home and see if Erna could secure a loan of $3,000 from the family. Erna didn't let him down and he had the money within a week.

From then on, everybody got paid and Henry took over the books. Bill continued to get the jobs all right but his work ethic didn't change. He showed up at ten in the morning and was gone before three in the afternoon. Another thing caught Henry's attention. In the middle of a job, Bill asked for more money, claiming that he had miscalculated the cost of the job they were doing. They were fortunate that the contractor didn't hold them to their contract and paid them the extra money requested. It happened a few times and it was a good thing they were the only large painting company on the island or they probably would have been thrown off the job.

Henry watched and learned and paid off his loan in record time. Bill wasn't happy. He told Henry it could wait until the following month. They were in their second year of business, and there was plenty of work, when someone asked him if he was aware that Bill had bought a horse for one of his daughters and that he often slipped away early in the afternoons to go riding. Henry had also lent his VW Beetle to Bill's wife, who totaled it when she ran a red light, and he never saw the vehicle again. Henry immediately knew it was time to find a way to dissolve the partnership and go off on his own.

When the next draw came for the job they were doing, Henry took the check and went to the Paint Locker to pay off what they owed for the month and closed his account. He told the owner that his association with Bill had ended and that he would no longer be responsible for anything Bill purchased from that moment on. Then he deducted his original investment and his paycheck for that week and handed the rest over to Bill and told him, "Here is where we part company."

He was sure Bill must have seen it coming but he didn't moved a muscle. Henry explained to him that there was enough money left to meet the next week's payroll and that he had taken care of the

Paint Locker bill and closed the account. There were no hard feelings and they both just realized they would be better off if they went their separate ways. Bill seemed happy with it. He knew Henry had let him off easy, considering the money he owed Henry but he just considered it payment, in full, for teaching him the painting trade. Henry informed him that he intended to keep the company name though, as everything had been done in his name. Bill seemed all right with it and they shook hands and walked away.

Henry made the rounds to all of their business contacts to let them know that his relationship with Bill had ended, for personal reasons, but he would appreciate the chance to bid on any upcoming work. It was an uncertain time but relief swept over him. It felt so good to be free and on his own again. Thankfully, by this time, he could read a blue print pretty well and was able to give estimates based on that. He put together a crew and approached the supervisors of new construction sites.

After six months, Bill found him and told him that he had just signed a contract for a three-story condo that was being built and he couldn't handle it for some reason. He told Henry that if he was interested in the job, he would sell him the contract for a "finder's fee" of $500. Henry agreed if the contract was signed over to his name. It turned out to be with one of the biggest construction firms on the island and there was no problem in the office with signing the contract over to the painting company. He gave Bill the check for the agreed upon amount and that was the beginning of a long and prosperous relationship with the construction company. Whether he realized it or not, Bill helped create his greatest competition with that contract sale.

After completing the job, the work kept rolling in but Henry knew his limitations and never took on more work than he could handle. In doing so, he built a reputation as someone who could be relied upon to start and finish the job as promised. He became aware that sometimes his bids were higher than the competition but he still got the contracts. Henry finally decided that it was time to settle down and build a house.

With the assistance of a real estate agent, Henry purchased three-quarters of an acre of land in the center of the island. He built a temporary structure on the side of the property so it wouldn't interfere with future house plans. He says this of his dwelling:

"This little plywood palace, ended up being eight feet wide and 24 feet long. Big enough to store all of my belongings and hold the mattress I bought on the frame that I built out of two by fours, window high, so that I was able to take full advantage of the trade winds. Windows consisted of a piece of wood propped up by a stick. The floor was of genuine native dirt, not to be swept, only sprinkled with water, to keep the dust down.

There were enough mosquitoes around that warranted the purchase of a mosquito net, and with that installed, with the window wide open, and me laying there and looking at the sky full of stars, really gave me a high. The only thing that was missing was the lion's roar, and I would have thought that I was on a safari in Africa.

I had no electricity, no running water, matter of fact; I had no water on the property at all. Eventually, I had a well dug, and water was found at 160 feet deep, but this was still two years away. My biggest problem was that the nearest power pole was about seven-hundred feet from my property, and the power company informed me that the first hundred feet was for free, and that for the rest of the distance, I would have to pay so much per foot out of my own pocket. It was not cheap either, but I coughed up the money, and still had to wait over a year before the power company finally installed the pole right on the edge of my property. It was quite a big subdivision, nothing smaller than three quarter acre lots, and when I bought, there could not have been more than a dozen houses standing.

I really had to tough it out all those months but being single at the time helped. Since I had brought a drop in four-burner gas range from New York, I built myself a table, cut out the center to fit the gas-range and my kitchen became almost operational, especially after I hooked up a 200-pound liquid gas tank that I had acquired from the gas company.

Since my shower was outside, I had to wait for it to get dark. The chamber pot consisted of a five-gallon empty paint can with a double paper brownbag for solid waste. Which I dumped every morning into the corner dumpster as I drove by on my way to work. Liquids were deposited into a hole that I had dug well away from my palatial dwelling. And I had to go through all this trouble since I was not allowed to put up an outhouse.

Almost forgot, for light in the evening I used a Coleman lantern that I had brought with me from the States. For water I filled up empty five-gallon paint buckets at the place wherever I happened to work, and it was not long before I had a reserve of a couple of hundred gallons accumulated of this precious commodity." (Stern, 2006)

Eventually Henry had a well and cistern system put in and then worked a deal with a contractor friend who sent some of his men over during dry spells to help erect a house as Henry was too busy with his business to work on it. The house took shape and he was finally able to move in. He built all of his own cabinets and cooked most of his own meals, but on Saturday nights he went out and ate a 16-inch pizza by himself. He also went to a movie once in a while and read books. Eventually, he even got electricity installed.

In the original building plans, Henry had designed a duplex each with one bedroom, a living room, a kitchen, and a bathroom. However, he ended up with a two-bedroom duplex that in the middle of construction, changed again. One side became two-stories with two bedrooms, a living room, a bathroom, a kitchen, and a dining room on one side, and the original one-story version on the side. This enabled him to move into the upstairs and rent out the other two units. Meanwhile, he added a one-car garage and 15 by 30-foot swimming pool with a three-foot deck surrounding it.

Henry did all of this despite being busy with his painting business, he could work seven days a week if the men working for him were willing to put in the time. However, he wasn't all work and no play.

"Before anybody starts feeling sorry for me, let me tell you that many a day, after starting the men off in the morning and having made sure that they had enough material for the day to work with, I disappeared now and then and spent an hour or so at the beach. When I was there, production was up. When I left, production dropped, but it was still acceptable as far as I was concerned. Then I went back to the worksite and worked with them for a while and then found an excuse to leave

them, telling them I'd be back shortly. Worked like a charm. After all, the only person I had to please was myself, and I lived my life accordingly." (Stern, 2006)

All in all, he liked the direction his life was going in, in 1969. He stayed busy with work, building his house, and studying Objectivism, which helped him to see that things are what they are and not what you want them to be. It helped him to learn a lot about himself and to see things in a more positive way. He made some friends and was content at last until out of the blue, he received a disturbing call from his mother.

Calling from New York, Erna's voice was filled with panic as she expressed to her son that when she returned home that afternoon she discovered, after entering, that her apartment had been ransacked. Someone had broken a window to gain entrance using the escape ladder that ran alongside the building. Furniture was upended, drawers pulled out and rifled through, and even the kitchen wasn't spared. After a cursory inspection, Erna noticed that there was nothing taken and the would-be-thief was most likely looking for money or jewelry.

The apartment was a mess and Erna called the police immediately, who eventually showed up and told her that the chances of them catching the thief were highly unlikely. They recommended she have someone install bars on the windows. She didn't want to go on living there in the fear of the burglar returning so she decided to stay at a friend's home until she could figure out what to do.

Henry interrupted her ranting and suggested she lock her apartment door and join him in St. Croix, he had plenty of room. He had intended her to stay only until she decided on her next course of action but didn't realize, at the time, what he had just gotten himself into.

The day before her departure, Erna called Henry with her flight information and asked him to pick her up at the airport. Once her flight arrived, and Henry saw the amount of luggage she had with her, he realized there was more to this trip than he had counted on and his mother soon filled him in on the plan.

The good news was that Erna had a good flight over. The bad news was that she had given up her apartment, sold all of her furniture, and gave most of the items that she couldn't take with her to her friends. The only thing she kept was her sewing machine, which she had shipped by regular mail and was on its way. Before Henry could say a word, his mother reminded him that he had offered her a home so there she was. He had expected a visitor but got a full-time resident.

There was plenty of room in the house and Erna moved into the guest bedroom and made herself right at home. It didn't take long before she began to take over. At first, Henry didn't mind because she cooked and cleaned and things ran smoothly for a while. He thought he had made it clear to his mother that he never knew when he would get home from work each night and if she chose to cook, not to expect him there at a certain time. He explained that even after work, his work continued. He had to prepare and make sure that there was enough material for the next day. He told her that if he felt like grabbing a bite to eat, he would. He told her that he appreciated all she was doing but she could just put the leftovers in the refrigerator and he would eat as and when he could. However, when she cooked dinners and he didn't show up "on time," she threw a fit. She would complain that he didn't appreciate all of the work she put into it. He reminded her time and time again that he couldn't commit to a schedule and that she didn't have to cook for him. If she felt like it, he could eat leftovers but old habits die hard and she kept cooking.

The house was about a mile from the main road and Erna could hail a taxi or hitch a ride to the places she wanted to go but once a week Henry would take her shopping and out to eat. When Henry had friends over for drinks, Erna fit right in. Henry and his mother even had some great discussions on Objectivism but she would never discuss the identity of his father and this strained their relationship and it remained so for the rest of her life.

Before long, the house was just getting too small for the two of them. Henry decided to build his mother a one-bedroom guesthouse on the edge of the property, near the pool. Erna loved the idea because she also realized that they each needed their own space. He contacted his contractor friend and the building got underway within two weeks. As the construction continued, tension between Henry and his mother built up faster than the guest house until finally his Aunt Roeschen from Berlin sent Erna a round-trip ticket asking her to come and visit for a while. She jumped at the chance and stayed in Berlin for about six weeks. Once she returned, her little house was almost finished.

In Erna's absence, things had changed on the home front. Dominique and Bonnie, friends of Henry's, had been trying to get him to meet a friend of Bonnie's. Apparently, Bonnie had a friend in the States who they felt would make the perfect partner for him. She was described as being a very pretty real blond, 5'3" and a really sweet person. She was intelligent and so on. Finally, after two years, her girlfriend was coming to the island. He never gave it much thought and had even forgotten about it when one day his doorbell rang. It was Dominique and Bonnie with her girlfriend Barbara in tow.

Bonnie hadn't exaggerated. Henry saw before him "a cute little thing, blond alright, and a good figure to boot." After introductions, Barbara informed him that she had been taking care of her mother for the past year and that after she passed away, decided to take Bonnie up her offer to come for a visit. They were in an interesting situation. They both knew something about the other before they had even met. Also, they both realized that they were being set up so they tried to play it cool. Neither of them felt sparks flying but there was some attraction and after a few drinks and polite conversation, they agreed to see each other again soon.

Three days later while driving down a back road into town, Henry noticed Dom and company coming in the opposite direction. They passed each other on the road. Each stopped their cars and backed up. Henry got out of his car and boldly approached Dom's car and asked Barbara if she would like to go to dinner that night. After picking her up that night for their date, life was never the same for either one of them again.

Barbara proved to be an excellent listener as Henry spoke

mostly of his love of living on the island and of his business but as he was still very much into the subject of Objectivism, he bored her with that as well. When he finally gave her the chance to speak he learned that she came from Scandinavian stock. Her mother and father had been born in the States but her grandparents on both sides had come from Sweden and settled in Marquette in Michigan. Barbara was the oldest child of four and had two brothers and a sister. Henry also learned that he was three months her senior. She went on to tell him of her deep need to get away, thus the trip to the island. The past year had been a tough one for her. When Henry asked her, what was next for her, she replied that as soon as she figured that out, she would let him know.

A comfortable relaxation swept over both of them. There was no tension, as if they had known each other forever. Not wanting to lose a moment of the weekend, they took advantage of the time they had by going dining and dancing but the weekend activities soon spilled into the next week and kept going from there. After three weeks of daily interaction, Henry asked Barbara to move in with him while she continued to decide what her next course in life was. She agreed and the next day they drove to Dom's house, where she had been staying, and picked up all of her belongings.

Naturally, Henry told Barbara about his mother having the next bedroom until the guest house was completed. He then wrote to Erna, who was still visiting with her sister in Germany. He explained that he had met a nice girl who was just his age and that she had moved in with him. He knew that Erna would make up her own mind about Barbara in the weeks to come.

Since everyone had been forewarned, nothing out of the ordinary happened when Erna finally returned from Germany and Henry introduced her to Barbara. Both ladies smiled politely, and Henry says, "That was that!" Despite Barbara's multiple offers, Erna politely rejected any help with the cooking or cleaning, which she had once again taken over since her return. Barbara, not being one to sit around idle, went into town and found a job at a lawyer's office for five days a week.

On weekends, they all went out to eat and because Erna didn't have much use for the beach, Henry and Barbara spent time there alone. Sometimes, Erna even had Henry drive her to a friend's house for the day. He was genuinely surprised by how smoothly everything was going. Then one day Barbara enlightened him. She admitted to always letting Erna have her way but once she moved into the guest house, she would start to rule the roost.

Finally, Erna's house was ready. The three of them shopped for furniture and décor and helped her make her little house into a home. She was quite happy to have a little place to call her own. Henry even convinced her to gain more independence by enrolling in a driving school so she could get her license and drive herself wherever she wanted to go.

Everything went smoothly for a while until Barbara received a phone call from her brother in Michigan, informing her that her father had been in an accident while hunting in Wyoming. While he was crossing the street, a car came out of nowhere and hit him, picking him up and throwing him over the top of the car. Miraculously, he was only a little banged up, so it wasn't serious. He had a few bruises and was shaken up but nothing was broken. Her brother thought it was a good idea for her to come home for a week or so to try and cheer the old man up. She took some time off work and headed home.

As soon as Barbara was out of the house, Erna felt it necessary to come up to the house very early in the morning, put on coffee and entice Henry into having some breakfast. He realized that she meant well but in those days he rarely ate anything in the morning. He assumes that his heavy smoking curbed his appetite. He began each day with two or three cups of coffee and that many, or more, cigarettes and generally didn't get hungry until around noon. He packed a sandwich and thermos of coffee every day for lunch except for the rare occasion when he went into town for a healthy lunch, sometimes with Barbara when she could break free from work.

Barb and Henry stayed in contact by phone while she was gone and before long, her father had improved enough that she felt she could return to St. Croix. He and Erna had come to a silent truce while Barb was away. She showed up at his house whenever she wanted to. At times she cooked and they ate together. It was peaceful and life was good.

Henry and Erna often took rides together around the island, during which times they talked a lot. Henry suggested that she find more to do with her time instead of just sitting home alone all the time. The topic of male companionship for her even came up, which again led to the question of his father. He tried to bring up the topic as objectively as he could by making it clear that he would never pass judgment in any way, shape, or form, and told her that all he wanted was the name of the donor. He stressed that he had the right to know. Clearly not getting anywhere, he addressed her directly by name, again pointing out that he wouldn't judge her, he had the right to know and he was only asking for a name. He stressed that he carried his grandfather's name proudly but every person had the right to know the people responsible for their presence here on Earth. Henry even tried humor by reminding Erna that the Immaculate Conception excuse had been used already and wouldn't work. This didn't even bring a smile to his mother's face.

In the long run, Henry states, "Erna was not as smart as I gave her credit for. Needless to say, our relationship didn't improve after this little encounter."

"When I think about it, I had started on that subject [his paternity] on and off since the day I had met her in 1940 but had never gotten anywhere, and this was 1973. That was the last time I approached that subject.

It took me a long time before it finally dawned on me why I never addressed Erna as Mother. I came to the conclusion that we are judged by our actions. To make a child or bear a child is not a parent to be. A dog can do the same thing, and you would not call them parents, even though the mother stays with her pups for the first six weeks until they are weaned. To be called a mother or father is a title that has to be earned." (Stern, 2006)

In the heat of Henry's conversation with Erna, things were said that led them to realize that the island of St. Croix wasn't big enough for the both of them. Erna gracefully volunteered to return to New York and it didn't take her long to pack her belongings. Henry promised to send the remaining items, that she couldn't take with her, just as soon as she could provide him with a forwarding address.

Henry made the reservation and within the week Erna returned to Brooklyn. He wasn't overly concerned about her as she knew many people there, although she didn't return to the unsafe neighborhood that she had fled from previously. A friend of hers took her in for a short time until she found a one-bedroom apartment across the street from her cousin. Later, Erna confessed that she was happy to get back to the old neighborhood where she had lived for so many years. St. Croix was just an interlude, an action of panic.

Barbara and Erna had gotten along fairly well but when Barb returned and Henry told her the reasons for Erna's departure, no tears were shed. She admitted that this was the best solution for all concerned. Barb's father had recovered from the accident and enjoyed the family get together. Henry would eventually meet them and he always enjoyed their company.

Barbara felt badly for the way Erna left the island so she kept encouraging Henry to call her to try and patch things up. He resisted for a while and was quite stubborn about it but he realized where that stubbornness came from. Eventually, Henry caved to Barb's persistent plea and he made the phone call. Once he did so, he was glad he did, knowing nothing is gained by not speaking to each other.

At one point, while Erna had still been living with Henry and Barbara, Erna confronted him and asked him why he and Barbara didn't just get married. She pointed out, "If after two and a half years, you still don't know if she's the right one for you, you'll never know."

Erna must have talked to Barbara too because the next week as Henry was just about to come out of the cistern after giving it another coat of waterproofing, he stuck his head out, and there stood Barbara looking at him. She began, "I don't think I want to stay here any longer. After two and a half years, I have reached a dead end just hanging around here."

At that moment, Henry realized that he didn't want to lose her and that he really loved her. Standing on the ladder with half of his body inside and half outside, he told her he loved her and wanted to marry her. He told her that if she still wanted to leave the island, he would go with her. Barb accepted his proposal and they set a wedding date for January 2. They made an appointment with the judge and Erna, Dom, and Bonnie served as witnesses. Henry recalls the day.

"The judge asked each of us "Will you, Henry," and "Will you, Barbara?" After saying their I dos, they were married. Henry says, "Single one moment, and within five minutes, life changed for the better, as far as I'm concerned. Please don't tell Barb I said that." Erna gave them a nice dinner party at the Top Hat restaurant in C-Sted (Christiansted). With that, another chapter of Henry's life began." (Stern, 2006)

On the work front, there were changes too. Henry had connected with a new contractor named Roy who came in from the States and who specialized in prefabricated concrete work. He constructed a few high-priced homes that way and made quite a splash when he landed a big job for a hotel on the eastern side of the island. He and Henry got to be friends. In one of their conversations Henry must have mentioned that, in addition to painting, he had done plumbing on the island as a licensed plumber because soon after that conversation, Roy had a business proposition for him. It got Henry thinking.

At that time, the island's economy was booming. There was a definite need for private homes. So, when Roy asked him if he'd be interested in a limited partnership in his construction firm, he was interested. Roy furthered his cause by pointing out that there was a construction boom going on and there was a lot of money to be made by putting up some spec houses. He wanted Henry's expertise in doing the plumbing and finish work.

Roy felt that by using the method of pre-casting the exterior wall at his construction yard and then transporting them to the site to be erected on the footings built beforehand, they could build those exterior walls quickly and efficiently. As it turned out, they were also hurricane proof. It seemed that Henry had forgotten his previous experiences with partnerships. Enthusiasm caused him to think that it sounded like an idea that was too good to pass up. For $20,000, he bought himself a limited partnership. He had come a long way in ten years. Beginning as a painter, then a painting contractor, and finally, the co-owner of a construction company.

Henry's new company acquired four building lots and they began to put up two-bedroom, two-bath homes. Henry did all of the plumbing, painting, and stuccoing. Everything went smoothly and without any problems until the last building lot. They arrived on a Monday morning to discover that all of the doors and windows were missing, along with the hot water heater and water pump. They called the police but very little was done.

Roy decided to contact Henry's former partner, Bill, who was, then, in the guard dog business and one was delivered. When they arrived the next morning, the dog had been left in the house. Apparently, Bill had forgotten to collect it on his daily rounds. When Roy entered the house the dog was quite happy to see him and slobbered all over him. When Bill finally arrived to retrieve his vicious canine, Roy told him to take his pussycat home and to not bother coming back. Henry found them a dog with a big bark that they put in the house at night and they never had another problem.

It was sad to see an island that had everything going for it begin to deteriorate from within. When Henry had arrived in St. Croix in 1961, he felt welcomed by the population. Slowly, as the population grew and tourism increased on the island, he detected a certain undercurrent of resentment from the locals.

Since the end of World War II, when the Caribbean Islands became easily accessible by plane, the tourist trade started to boom. People fell in love with the islands where the climate is an easy 72 to 92 degrees year-round with trade winds to cool you off. People bought land, opened new businesses, hired local help and built themselves the dream houses they had always wanted. Supply and demand drove prices up over the years. Interestingly, most of the land was owned by about five island families who, before the convenience of the airplanes, were land rich but money poor, but not for long.

Hotels and condominiums sprang up all over the island and with the influx of people from the mainland the locals became resentful. The government tried to keep up with the growing population. New schools were constructed and a new hospital was erected. Not long after was the construction of the V.I. College. In other words, the island of St. Croix was growing and so was the resentment of some of the Cruzan people toward the Continentals, until one day in September, 1972, when things drastically changed.

On that day, a small band of five men, who were later identified as belonging to some kind of a sect of Rastafarian rebel rousers, stormed out of the bushes dressed in military camouflage at the Fountain Valley Golf Course. Armed with automatic rifles, they opened fire, shooting indiscriminately at anything that moved. Some of the tourists who were sitting at the bar having drinks got hit. The entire episode couldn't have taken more than a moment or so but before anyone could figure out what had happened, the men fled back into the woods and vanished.

In total, seven people died and a few were wounded. The next day, the story ran in all of the newspapers. Headlines read, "St. Croix Fountain Valley Massacre." Media from all over the United States picked up on the story and some headlines called St. Croix "Murder Island."

Marshalls from the mainland came over to help with the investigation and it wasn't long before all of the perpetrators were apprehended, tried, and convicted. Henry doesn't recall how many years they actually served in prison but he says the one of the outgoing governors decided to pardon them as he was leaving office. Bitterly, Henry points out, "While the victims rot in the ground, those murderers roam around free as birds. So much for Cruzan justice."

Tourism dropped to nothing and the bottom fell out of the economy in St. Croix. Henry had to wonder what purpose any of this served. It was a small faction of disgruntled locals who wanted to overthrow the existing government and declare themselves the new rulers so they could govern and run the island as Haiti had been for the last 200 years.

Even many of the old-timers, who had lived on the island for years, just packed up and left the island for good. Henry and Roy had just finished their four spec houses when this event occurred and as you might have guessed, those new homes sat empty for a long time. The market just collapsed and it took them a long time to sell them. They were lucky to get their investment back.

Henry found some positive in the situation though. At least he had learned a lot about construction. Things turned out much worse for Roy. Not long after those events, his doctor told him that he had lung cancer. Due to circumstances beyond their control, the two men decided to dissolve their partnership. Roy gave Henry his original investment back and he got to keep the truck he had been using.

Things were slow for a while but Henry kept busy with repeat business and an occasional plumbing repair job, enough to still make a decent living. By 1978, however, Henry was only doing small repairs and repaint jobs. The bread and butter jobs had dried up and St. Croix's economy wasn't showing any signs of recovery so he and Barbara started talking about putting the house on the market and going to Florida to retire.

Selling their home took over a year but eventually they sold it to a missionary lady from the States. Henry and Barbara sold the house completely furnished, with everything in it except for a few personal belongings, which they shipped to Florida and they took the next plane out.

Henry had mixed emotions about leaving an island he had loved and called home for more years than any other place he had lived in before. Change would be good though, he thought. Everyone needs change once in a while. One thing bothered Henry and it was their age. They were only 50 years old, a bit young to retire but as he puts it, "What the Hell. If we don't like it, we can always go back into business or find a job."

26

THE WELL DESERVED EXTENDED VACATION

The Sterns, Henry, Barbara, and their miniature poodle Shoo-Shoo, arrived back in the States and were temporarily staying with a friend of theirs, one of two men who had rented out one of their St. Croix units, in Hollywood. They were looking for a place in Miami but found it to be too congested and decided it was a good time to drive around and see the country.

After renting a storage unit for the belongings they shipped from the island, they bought a Chevy van and converted it into a motor home. It had a queen-sized bed, portable toilet, a dresser, and it served as their home for the next three months. In it they traveled to the Grand Canyon, Yellowstone Park, Bryce National Park, the Mesa Verde, and Mount Rushmore. They also saw the Grand Tetons and the Badlands of the Dakotas.

When they reached Phoenix, Barb came up with the idea of calling Erna in New York to invite her to join them on their trip to Las Vegas. Henry called her and Erna arrived the very next day. They picked her up at Phoenix Airport and were on their way. They stopped at the Grand Canyon for the day and then headed to Vegas.

The three of them stayed in Vegas for three days. Not much for gambling, Henry and Barbara left only losing only $20 between them. Erna, however, loved to gamble. Henry never saw her happier than "when she pulled that one-armed bandit." She actually left Vegas with a few extra bucks. When the three days were up, Erna flew back to New York with a smile on her face.

The trip for Henry and Barbra, which they called their "safari" went on. After more than three months, they decided to head back to Florida to see if they could find a place to settle down in and live happily ever after. That was easier said than done. They drove both coastlines with no definite place in mind. That's when Henry remembered that someone he used to know lived in Sarasota, a nice place so they decided to give that a try.

After finding his phone number, Henry gave the man a call. He remembered Henry right away and told him to come on over. Following a conversation with him, they decided to rent a place for a week and by the end of it, they were the proud owners of a prefabricated home in Ellenton, not far from the Manatee River, in the town of Bradenton.

As he feared, it didn't take long before the two Sterns got bored. Barbara found herself a job within walking distance from where they lived, as a sales lady in a upmarket dress shop. Henry went back to what he knew best, painting. He had no problem finding a job. He was hired on the spot by the first contractor he approached and after a couple of jobs, he met and worked with a native Floridian (yes, they do exist) who asked him if he would be interested in going it alone. Since there was nothing to sign, he decided to give it a try.

The two men teamed up and before long, they landed a big job painting six duplexes. The contractor informed them that unless they came down on their per-unit price, he would replace them with others who worked for less. As there was only a verbal contract and because the money hadn't been that great anyway, Henry told him to have a lousy life, and departed.

Henry soon discovered the problem was that for every job that went out for bids, there were at least six guys salivating while trying to get it. Painting was a cut-throat business in Florida.

After living in Florida for two years, Henry and Barbara talked it over and decided to go back to St. Croix, at least for a little while.

He didn't expect much improvement business-wise but it was the only place he had ever lived where he was truly happy. Being the understanding wife that she was, Barb understood his reasons for wanting to return to St. Croix. They realized that this stay would be temporary and that made it easier to face what was to come.

Packing all of the necessary equipment for the painting trade into the back of his truck had almost become routine. They called their friends Dom and Bonnie and asked for their help in finding a place to live. Fortunately, they discovered that the couple had rental units and one would be available for them. They were able to move in right away.

Once settled into their new one-bedroom dwelling, they picked up their truck with all of their belongings from the dockside. While Barbara started to get organized and stored their personal items away, Henry went out and made the rounds and looked up all of the people he had done business with before. They all wondered what had become of him and where he had been hiding. He told them that he had been on a, well-deserved, extended vacation but he was back and looking for work now. It didn't take long before he was back in business. Construction had in fact started to pick up on the island again and soon he had his fair share of work. He was able to rehire some of the men who had worked for him previously and it felt like he had never even left.

It had been almost ten years since the killings had taken place. People hadn't forgotten but as someone once told Henry, "Whatever happens here on St. Croix, the almost perfect year-round climate will bring people back in the hopes that one can co-exist with the native population." That seemed to ring true based on the construction upswing he was seeing.

Soon, the feeling that something was missing started to nag at Henry. He realized that it had to do with not having his own place to live. He didn't like having to pay rent so he decided to, once again, build his own home from the ground up. He found a nice half-acre lot about three minutes from their rental. It had what he calls, "a view to kill for." He had the bulldozer slice a platform into the hill for the foundation and he went to work.

During the day the painting business was Henry's priority but as soon as he got home and finished dinner, he went up to the site to work on the house. Thinking back now, he doesn't know what possessed him to start the big undertaking of building a house almost completely by himself. He hired occasional help for certain jobs but did most of it on his own. It was a challenge but one that was fun to do.

As usual, the house Henry originally visualized and the one he ended up with were two very different things. Basically, the upstairs ended up being a three-bed, two-bath, with a kitchen, full dining room, living room, and entrance hall. Downstairs, consisted of a bedroom, a bathroom, kitchen with eating area and a nice-sized living room. He was also able to squeeze in an efficiency apartment downstairs.

Once Henry had the shell for the house up, which took about a year to complete, he and Barbara moved in upstairs. It took him another year to complete the project. He rented the other two units almost immediately. From there, he began work on a swimming pool with a cabana. He also constructed a 10 by 20 workshop and a two-car carport. He had proven to himself that he could build a house with minimal help. All it took was a lot of sweat and the end result was a great feeling of pride and accomplishment.

While Henry built, Barbara got bored so she took a job in town selling whatever tourists would buy. Their friend Bonnie had tried her hand at various enterprises and had opened and closed many shops until she settled into selling health-related products and operating a beauty shop. She suggested to Barbara, on several occasions, that she should open a store of her own.

There was an empty store near Bonnie's business and eventually Barb decided to use it for a shop specializing in islands curios. She called it Fun in the Sun. It did quite well this venture of her own kept Barb busy. With both of them staying so active, the years flew by.

The Sterns always made time to go on vacation twice a year, either to New York to see Henry's family or to Michigan to see Barb's. Henry had just finished up a painting job when he received a phone call from New York and to come back right away because Erna was sick. He went back immediately and stayed with her for a couple of weeks. He was unable to do anything for her but stayed until Erna told him to go back to Barbara and promised to call him if she needed him.

Everything was fine for a while when Erna's cousin called him and suggested he come back to Erna. He told her he would catch the next plane. This time, Barb went with him and it was a good thing she did. Three weeks later, Erna lost her battle with pancreatic cancer. He was never able to communicate with her further and she died with the secret of his father's identity. He had her cremated and spread her ashes in a place she dearly loved, Sheep's Head Bay in Brooklyn. The carefree times that Henry had loved so much were over.

With all of the problems that St. Croix once had, the economy started to improve. He and Barb had a good life. They had made it. Both had their businesses, were making good money, and had a beautiful home so he has no idea what made them decide to put their house on the market and go back to the States. Maybe they just wanted more out of life. It took them a while to sell their home but eventually it sold and for a good price. Again, they said their goodbyes. He wondered if anyone put bets on when or if they would return again.

27

GOING TO AMERICA 1988

The Sterns left the island of St. Croix, for good this time. As it turned out, they did so just in time. The following year, the island was hit by Hurricane Hugo, one of the largest hurricanes ever. It devastated the island to the point, he was later told by an eye witness, that by the time the storm was over, there wasn't one blade of green grass left to be seen and the ground had turned brown. It took years for the island's flora to recover and regrow.

Once, Henry and Barbara had a one-day stopover there in 1998 on a cruise they had taken around the Caribbean Islands but things had really changed on the island. There was a brand new four-lane highway, which replaced the old Centerline Road connecting Christiansted with Frederiksted. The big store of little Switzerland was downsized to a shadow of its former size, even though the original building they were in wasn't touched by the hurricane but anything that wasn't nailed down was looted. Many of the stores never reopened after that.

The island just wasn't the same as Henry remembered it. When he first stepped on the island in 1961, the population was about 10,000 people. By 2002, not too many years after that one-day stop, it was up to about 60,000.

Toward the end of their stay, Henry and Barbara became

acutely aware of the deterioration of the goodwill of the islanders. The innocent charm with which the natives used to greet you was gone with the exception of the older generation. "We liked it better with less. With all of the progress came crime, more guns than the island had ever seen, dope being peddled openly and hate amongst the islanders."

The move back to the States went smoothly. They were pros at it by that stage. Once again, their loaded vehicles were shipped to Miami. After looking around, they no longer cared for Ellenton, where they had settled previously. They decided to settle down in Sarasota. A few people they knew from the island were there and it didn't take them long to find a home that suited their needs. It was a nice house in a good neighborhood. It needed a little fixing, so Henry knew, "It was right up my alley." The house was big enough and he just couldn't resist converting a small part of it into a one-bedroom rental unit. They had no problem renting it and they used the money to travel and see if there were greener pastures to settle in.

First, they looked in Upstate New York, then New Jersey, and Connecticut. It was fun looking around but they never really saw anything that they liked better than what they already had. So, they headed back to Sarasota where they stayed for the next two years. Then Barbara's younger sister convinced them to try her area, Colorado Springs. She bugged them about it often, insisting they would love it, so as you might have guessed they moved on and gave it a try.

Before selling the house, Henry bought a trailer with a 3,500-pound load capacity. They packed it to the hilt with all of their belongings, including some furniture. They tired of buying new things every time they moved. On the way, they sang their theme song, Willie Nelson's "On the Road Again."

It took them about four days to reach Colorado Springs and Barb's sister Kay was quite happy to see them arrive. She had a beautiful house with views of Pike's Peak, three bedrooms and a lot more house with a huge mortgage. She was also in the process of divorcing her husband. They had come at a good time.

Enamored with the Rocky Mountains and beautiful vistas, Henry and Barb decided to give it a try. They stayed as paying guests, which they felt was the right thing to do. Before long though, Barb's sister realized that she couldn't manage the house after her husband moved out and she decided to put it up for sale. Vowing to remain single, she was ready to move on.

Henry says that resolution didn't last long. Within three weeks his sister-in-law introduced them to her new beau. She had met him by answering an ad in the newspaper. He was a divorced man and retired from a 26-year military career with the Air Force. Once the house sold they moved into a more affordable apartment. They were married after about six months.

Henry and Barbara rented a two-bedroom place while hoping to find and buy a house within their budget. They managed to survive their first winter pretty well. After having lived on St. Croix for so many years, the winter was certainly different. With the assistance of a real estate agent, they looked at home after home but none of them met their needs so they began to drive all over the state of Colorado, visiting Vail, Aspen, and Cripple Creek, and they spent quality time with their nephews. Soon though, they were grateful that they hadn't found the perfect home.

With the second winter setting in, they both realized, as Henry describes it, "Those bones of ours preferred to bleach in the sun than to have our marrow freeze solid. And who are we to deny them the comfort of a sunny day and a good swim in the ocean in January?"

After a snowfall in April, they reloaded their trailer, said goodbye to the family and then hit the road again. They took their time driving back to Florida and even though they had no place in particular to go to, they were in good spirits.

In 1994, Henry along with his wife, Barbara, were on the road again. Even to them, it seemed ridiculous. Almost middle-aged, they still couldn't seem to settle down. They arrived in St. Petersburg only to be reminded of the harsh humidity so they landed in St. Augustine where they found a spot to unhook their trailer for a while until they found a place they liked.

Unfortunately, it was too touristy for them. Next, they tried the Panhandle of Florida.

They came to Destin, once a small fishing village, and eight miles beyond that they found a place called Santa Rosa Beach. Nearby, they found a two-bedroom mobile home in a retirement village. After making the down payment and signing papers they had to wait eight weeks to move in so they used that time to go see Barbara's brother in Michigan. He had a cabin out in the woods that Henry and Barbara used, despite the fact that it had no electricity, running water, or inside plumbing. There was an outhouse and gaslights. It had a gas stove and they had plenty of five-gallon cans for water, which they filled up at her brother's house. But the place was idyllic. It was peaceful with just the woods around them and the river flowed within a 100 yards from the house. They even had a canoe to paddle down the river with whenever they wanted.

After five weeks, they drove to Manhattan and stayed at Henry's cousin's hotel for the remaining weeks until they could take possession of their new home. That gave them the chance to visit with his family. Then they headed back to Florida where they lived comfortably until Hurricane Opal.

As the storm approached, they had to flee the home and everything in it in the middle of the night. They drove all the way to Dothan, Alabama, and once the roads were passable a few days later, they returned to Florida to see what was left of their home. Expecting the worst, they were pleasantly surprised to see very little damaged but after another two years of storms that were too close for comfort, they decided a change of atmosphere was in order. They took a ride to Ocala, horse country, which had rolling hills and farms just north of central Florida and away from oceans. They liked what they saw. There, they found another retirement community and bought a three-bedroom and two-bathroom home. They sold the place in Santa Rosa and moved in.

Although it didn't seem like it would ever happen and even though they have taken several cruises and flights to exotic places,

Henry and Barbara finally settled down in their Shangri-la in Ocala, Florida.

It's there where I visited them and where Henry proudly showed his art and sculptures to me. It was here that he let me have just a glimpse inside his mind as he asked my opinion of one of his abstract paintings. "Not at all my favorite art style," I answered honestly when he asked what I saw in it. I, almost apologetically, responded that I saw the chaos of an unsettled mind. While the colors were quite pretty it almost felt, to me, like someone screaming out in pain. I was afraid of hurting him with my opinion but I wanted to see past his banter and bluntness to the lost little boy inside. I think I was on to something because he indicated that I had hit the nail on the head.

During this visit, we sat and talked about his Holocaust experiences, his many moves over the years and shared our views on current issues and politics. Barbara was clearly the best partner that he could have chosen. She was pleasant, agreeable, and a calming presence in the room. Although Henry still had some of his stutter, clearly it had vastly improved over the years and the conversation flowed easily. His English was easy to understand, more so in talking than in his writing, as I would later discover in the hundreds of pages of writing he bestowed upon me but then that is what he wanted me to help him achieve in telling this story. He made it clear that it was up to me to take his experiences and share them with you in an easy to read format. I have loved getting to know him from his writing, his emails, and our visits.

AFTERWORD

While young Horst avoided incarceration in any concentration camp and bears no numbers on his arm, his life was forever changed during the Holocaust. From the first shattering of storefront windows and the burning of his school and synagogue during Kristallnacht in November, 1938, to the day the Soviets rolled through Budapest, he fought for survival.

Through cold and starvation, life in filthy ghettos, and forced hard labor and death marches, surviving on grass and as he calls it "hot water soup with a few rodent bones floating in it," Horst struggled to merely exist and carried the burden of bearing a man's responsibilities while still a boy. He managed to provide for his mother and grandmother, despite the odds that were stacked against them.

Regardless of how many books I read or how much I study the Holocaust, and antisemitism in general, I cannot wrap my mind around the extreme hatred that could pave the road for the kind of treatment that Horst's family, and so many others, endured. I cannot understand a hatred that could justify the death of even one person, let alone of the magnitude of the Holocaust.

Young Horst lived through hell. There is no other way to put it. He suffered and starved and for what? It was simply because of the religion into which he was born. His biological father, whoever he might be, wasn't even Jewish. Yet, Horst suffered at the hands of the Nazis for years. You might think that his suffering ended with the liberation toward the end of World War II. Yet, despite his light-hearted banter, some of the writing he shared with me that

wasn't included in his autobiography, indicates otherwise. I felt his frustration and bitterness, in part that he was treated as he was but in part because no one published one of his letters or even acknowledged them. I wish to acknowledge it in print here, so you too might feel his struggle.

"Going Down Memory Lane" - Henry Stern, December 20, 2013.

I have sent this letter to various German Magazines in Berlin, Germany! Needless to say, that none had the guts to acknowledge ever receiving it. None of them were ever returned to sender. Certain things one never forgets.

WHY?

Why did you start to persecute me when I was only five years old?

Why did your young bullies chase me down the street and beat me up just for not fitting the picture of how a real Aryan should look like? By then, I was only seven years old.

When I reached ten, you burned down my house of worship including my school of learning. That not being enough for one night, you had to break the glass of all Jewish owned store windows. That was November 9 and 10 in 1938.

Today it is known worldwide that there was such a thing as the night of breaking glass, better known as "Kristallnacht." That was only the beginning.

When I walked to school that November morning in 1938 in Berlin, Germany, and saw the pavement covered in glass and German citizens exiting those stores, taking everything that was not nailed down, I realized history was being made. I was only ten years old. I also remember the police standing there laughing and egging on the population telling them to take everything there for the owners of these stores would not need any of it where they were going.

On the Nights of November 9 and 10, gangs of Nazis roamed through Berlin Jewish neighborhoods breaking the windows of Jewish businesses and homes, burning synagogues. All in all, 101 synagogues and almost 7,500 Jewish businesses were destroyed. 26,000 Jews were arrested and sent to concentration camps, Jews were physically attacked and beaten and 91 died.

That was 1938. And I was only ten years old.

I lost many friends that year and from that time on. Mostly deported to Poland and to Germany, many as long as 30 years ago.

Needless to say, that was also the year my formal education ended. By the time I was 12 years old, we had escaped to Budapest, Hungary and just in time, too. If we had waited another day, the Gestapo (German secret police) would have picked us up to be interred into a concentration camp.

You followed us by invading Hungary in 1944 and continued trying to finish the job that you had sworn to do, namely; exterminate us all.

I was 16 years old when your bullies picked me up and put me into a slave labor camp.

Systematically, you decimated us. You worked us until most of the elderly died of exhaustion, and those who just could not produce enough work, you shot.

Then came the Death March on the road from Budapest to the Austrian border. End of the line was a concentration camp in Mauthausen or camp Auschwitz to be killed and cremated, or if you looked strong enough, you might have ended up in a Vienna War Factory (Austria) doing slave labor.

I did escape the transport and ended up in the Budapest Ghetto. You almost succeeded in killing me there. I had to disguise myself and play the role of an ugly girl that had not had a bath and stank to high heaven. It worked to a degree. I was never looked at twice.

However, I did survive.

The Russians liberated me on January 17, 1945. I was all of 17 years old.

You have decimated this world by 6 million Jews, over 60 years ago.

There are 6 million letters floating around with only one question that they want you to answer.

WHY?

As I worked on rewriting this book for Henry, I was

overwhelmed with sadness as the result of a horrific attack during its writing. An armed gunman entered a synagogue in Pittsburg, Pennsylvania, and killed 11 Jewish worshippers and wounded two others. He also wounded four law enforcement officers. All of this was done as he spewed antisemitic rants such as "All Jews must die." This isn't Nazi-era Europe. This was 2018 in the United States of America and it makes me absolutely sick to know that this type of extreme hatred still exists.

I can't wrap my mind around why. Why are the Jews so hated? Why should innocent people pay the price for that hatred? Shouldn't people learn from the Holocaust? Yet, it continues. It's sickening. It's a large part of why I have chosen to work with survivors like Henry, to make sure that the world knows what he suffered for in the name of hatred long after he is gone.

After having met Henry and Barbara, I'm not convinced that suffering has ever ended for Henry. Despite his jokes and laughter, I sense pain behind the smiles. I was exhausted just reading, in his original book, of his many moves and again in the rewriting. I felt it would never end. I felt that he was forever running. Was he running from something, inner demons perhaps? Or was he running in search of something? Was he seeking security? Answers? Peace? Whatever it is, I'm not convinced he has found it yet. How sad it must be to never feel settled.

Oh, he and Barbara have stayed put in their Ocala mobile home for a while but I think it's only age and health concerns that have finally put a halt to the transiency. Henry has found a form of escape in his unique wood sculptures and paintings but I wonder as he ages and is forced to stand still if the memories of all he experienced and all he lost now haunt his quiet mind.

When he turned all his writings over to me, he told me he did his best to tell his story but now it was my turn to try. In the case of some of the other Holocaust survivors I have known, the older they get, the worse the memories get. It seems that from their eighties to nineties, they relive their experiences more often and to the point that their sleep is often disturbed. I have the feeling that's why Henry asked me to take all of this off his hands. I know that it was beginning to cause him great stress but it was vital to him that his story be told.

As I finish putting the final touches on this book, I hope I have fulfilled my promise to the Sterns to retell the story of Horst's (Henry's) remarkable Holocaust survival. I can never truly express how honored I am that Henry trusted me to rewrite it, and bigger yet, trusted me to do so and then walked away from the project. I'm not sure that I have ever had such full faith placed in me. And if you, the reader, remember his story and the lessons we should learn from his, and other Holocaust survivors' experiences, than I will have done my job and you will fulfill Henry's strongest wishes. I hope I have done him justice and that this version of his story will serve as a legacy that he is proud to leave.

PHOTOGRAPHS

A sample of Henry's conversations with God

Henry's sculpture of the Twin Towers at his home - April 2015

Henry Stern in his home studio - April 2015

Henry and Debbie J. Callahan on Holocaust Remembrance Day, Ocala, Florida 2015. Photo credit: Michele Klopfenstein

ABOUT THE AUTHOR

Debbie J. Callahan resides with her husband Scott, and the greatest cat in the world, Calvin, in Downeast Maine. Callahan is a high school teacher instructing English and Exploring the Holocaust through Film and Literature.

Over the years, she has worked with Holocaust survivors and liberators, and volunteered at a Holocaust center. Additionally, she worked alongside the mayor of her city to coordinate Holocaust Remembrance events. She now devotes much of her time to writing and teaching about the importance of Holocaust Remembrance and Education.

Her books and lectures focus on everything from the danger of hatred, racism, and Antisemitism, to fighting Holocaust denial and the personal responsibility of sharing the stories of survivors, rescuers, liberators, and victims for future generations. In doing so, she fulfills her promise to survivors that their stories will not die with them and they will not be forgotten. Callahan writes and speaks to assure those who died at the hands of the Nazis did not die as statistics, numbers of dehumanized, faceless victims. She tells instead the stories of people who lived, worked, and loved; thus, sharing the humanity and legacies for generations to come.

The author can be contacted for presentations or book readings through: LegacyWriter68@gmail.com

* * *

If you have enjoyed reading my book,
please do leave a review on Amazon or Goodreads. A few kind words would be enough. This would be greatly appreciated.

Alternatively, if you read my book as Kindle eBook you could
simply leave a rating.
That is just one simple click,
indicating how many stars of five
you think this book deserves.
This will only cost you a split second.

Thank you very much in advance!

Debbie J. Callahan

AMSTERDAM PUBLISHERS HOLOCAUST LIBRARY

The series **Holocaust Survivor Memoirs World War II** consists of the following autobiographies of survivors:

The Dead Years. Holocaust Memoirs, by Joseph Schupack

Hank Brodt Holocaust Memoirs. A Candle and a Promise, by Deborah Donnelly

Rescued from the Ashes. The Diary of Leokadia Schmidt, Survivor of the Warsaw Ghetto, by Leokadia Schmidt

My Lvov. Holocaust Memoir of a twelve-year-old Girl, by Janina Hescheles

Remembering Ravensbrück. From Holocaust to Healing, by Natalie Hess

Wolf. A Story of Hate, by Zeev Scheinwald with Ella Scheinwald

Save my Children. An Astonishing Tale of Survival and its Unlikely Hero, by Leon Kleiner with Edwin Stepp

Holocaust Memoirs of a Bergen-Belsen Survivor & Classmate of Anne Frank, by Nanette Blitz Konig

Defiant German - Defiant Jew. A Holocaust Memoir from inside the Third Reich, by Walter Leopold with Les Leopold

In a Land of Forest and Darkness. The Holocaust Story of two Jewish Partisans, by Sara Lustigman Omelinski

Holocaust Memories. Annihilation and Survival in Slovakia, by Paul Davidovits

From Auschwitz with Love. The Inspiring Memoir of Two Sisters' Survival, Devotion and Triumph Told by Manci Grunberger Beran & Ruth Grunberger Mermelstein, by Daniel Seymour

Remetz. Resistance Fighter and Survivor of the Warsaw Ghetto, by Jan Yohay Remetz

My March Through Hell. A Young Girl's Terrifying Journey to Survival, by Halina Kleiner with Edwin Stepp

Roman's Journey, by Roman Halter

Beyond Borders. Escaping the Holocaust and Fighting the Nazis. 1938-1948, by Rudi Haymann

The Engineers. A memoir of survival through World War II in Poland and Hungary, by Henry Reiss

Spark of Hope. An Autobiography, by Luba Wrobel Goldberg

Footnote to History. From Hungary to America. The Memoir of a Holocaust Survivor, by Andrew Laszlo

Farewell Atlantis. Recollections, by Valentīna Freimane

The Courtyard. A memoir, by Benjamin Parket and Alexa Morris

The Mulberry Tree. The story of a life before and after the Holocaust, by Iboja Wandall-Holm

The Boy in the Back. A True Story of Survival in Auschwitz and Mauthausen, as told to Fern Lebo by Jan Blumenstein

Beneath the Lightless Sky. Surviving the Holocaust in the Sewers of Lvov, by Ignacy Chiger

From Sorrow to Joy. From Hitler's Darkness to the Sunlight on Mount Carmel, by Dr. Yakov Adler

Memories of a Subhuman. A Jewish Teenager's Journey of Survival. From Riga to Buchenwald and Back, by Aleksandr Bergman

The Kapos of Auschwitz, by Charles Liblau

The series **Holocaust Survivor True Stories** consists of the following biographies:

Among the Reeds. The true story of how a family survived the Holocaust, by Tammy Bottner

A Holocaust Memoir of Love & Resilience. Mama's Survival from Lithuania to America, by Ettie Zilber

Living among the Dead. My Grandmother's Holocaust Survival Story of Love and Strength, by Adena Bernstein Astrowsky

Heart Songs. A Holocaust Memoir, by Barbara Gilford

Shoes of the Shoah. The Tomorrow of Yesterday, by Dorothy Pierce

Hidden in Berlin. A Holocaust Memoir, by Evelyn Joseph Grossman

Separated Together. The Incredible True WWII Story of Soulmates Stranded an Ocean Apart, by Kenneth P. Price, Ph.D.

The Man Across the River. The incredible story of one man's will to survive the Holocaust, by Zvi Wiesenfeld

If Anyone Calls, Tell Them I Died. A Memoir, by Emanuel (Manu) Rosen

The House on Thrömerstrasse. A Story of Rebirth and Renewal in the Wake of the Holocaust, by Ron Vincent

Dancing with my Father. His hidden past. Her quest for truth. How Nazi Vienna shaped a family's identity, by Jo Sorochinsky

The Story Keeper. Weaving the Threads of Time and Memory - A Memoir, by Fred Feldman

Krisia's Silence. The Girl who was not on Schindler's List, by Ronny Hein

Defying Death on the Danube. A Holocaust Survival Story, by Debbie J. Callahan with Henry Stern

A Doorway to Heroism. A decorated German-Jewish Soldier who became an American Hero, by W. Jack Romberg

The Shoemaker's Son. The Life of a Holocaust Resister, by Laura Beth Bakst

The Redhead of Auschwitz. A True Story, by Nechama Birnbaum

Land of Many Bridges. My Father's Story, by Bela Ruth Samuel Tenenholtz

Creating Beauty from the Abyss. The Amazing Story of Sam Herciger, Auschwitz Survivor and Artist, by Lesley Ann Richardson

On Sunny Days We Sang. A Holocaust Story of Survival and Resilience, by Jeannette Grunhaus de Gelman

Painful Joy. A Holocaust Family Memoir, by Max J. Friedman

I Give You My Heart. A True Story of Courage and Survival, by Wendy Holden

In the Time of Madmen, by Mark A. Prelas

Monsters and Miracles. Horror, Heroes and the Holocaust, by Ira Wesley Kitmacher

Flower of Vlora. Growing up Jewish in Communist Albania, by Anna Kohen

Aftermath: Coming of Age on Three Continents. A Memoir, by Annette Libeskind Berkovits

Not a real Enemy. The True Story of a Hungarian Jewish Man's Fight for Freedom, by Robert Wolf

Zaidy's War. Four Armies, Three Continents, Two Brothers. One Man's Impossible Story of Endurance, by Martin Bodek

The Glassmaker's Son. Looking for the World my Father left behind in Nazi Germany, by Peter Kupfer

The Apprentice of Buchenwald. The True Story of the Teenage Boy Who Sabotaged Hitler's War Machine, by Oren Schneider

Good for a Single Journey, by Helen Joyce

Burying the Ghosts. She escaped Nazi Germany only to have her life torn apart by the woman she saved from the camps: her mother, by Sonia Case

American Wolf. From Nazi Refugee to American Spy. A True Story, by Audrey Birnbaum

Bipolar Refugee. A Saga of Survival and Resilience, by Peter Wiesner

In the Wake of Madness. My Family's Escape from the Nazis, by Bettie Lennett Denny

Before the Beginning and After the End, by Hymie Anisman

I Will Give Them an Everlasting Name. Jacksonville's Stories of the Holocaust, by Samuel Cox

Hiding in Holland. A Resistance Memoir, by Shulamit Reinharz

The Ghosts on the Wall. A Grandson's Memoir of the Holocaust, by Kenneth D. Wald

Thirteen in Auschwitz. My grandmother's fight to stay human, by Lauren Meyerowitz Port

The Jewish Woman Who Fought the Nazis. Bep Schaap-Bedak's life during the Holocaust in Holland, by Eli Schaap

Little Edna's War. A True story of Resistance and Hope. A Gripping WWII page-turner, by Janet Bond Brill, PhD

Voices of Resilience. An Anthology of Stories written by Children of Holocaust Survivors, Edited by Deborah (Devora) Ross-Grayman

Was it just a matter of luck? A Family, the Holocaust, and the Founding of a Museum, by Dr Charles Kaner

Dreaming of the River. A Mother and Daughter's Fight for Survival during the Holocaust, by Pauline Steinhorn

From One Generation to the Next. Unbroken Resilience, by Hymie Anisman

Irmgard. The Girl from Dresden. A Memoir of Survival and Legacy, by Fiona Kelmann

The World has Caught Fire, by Leah Grisham PhD

The series **Holocaust Heritage** consists of the following memoirs by 2G:

The Cello Still Sings. A Generational Story of the Holocaust and of the Transformative Power of Music, by Janet Horvath

The Fire and the Bonfire. A Journey into Memory, by Ardyn Halter

The Silk Factory: Finding Threads of My Family's True Holocaust Story, by Michael Hickins

Winter Light. The Memoir of a Child of Holocaust Survivors, by Grace Feuerverger

Out from the Shadows. Growing up with Holocaust Survivor Parents, by Willie Handler

Hidden in Plain Sight. A Family Memoir and the Untold Story of the Holocaust in Serbia, by Julie Brill

The Unspeakable. Breaking my family's silence surrounding the Holocaust, by Nicola Hanefeld

Eighteen for Life. Surviving the Holocaust,
    by Helen Schamroth

Four Survivor Grandparents. Run. Rely. Rebuild, by Jonathan Schloss

Austrian Again. Reclaiming a Lost Legacy,
    by Anne Hand

Never Fitting In. My Journey with Parental Trauma, Addiction, Healing, by Sonia Claire Ascher

Divine Corners. In the Shadow of the Holocaust on a Catskills Chicken Farm, by Michelle Friedman

Milk in an Eggshell. A WWII story of hiding in plain sight, by Miryam Sas

www.ingramcontent.com/pod-product-compliance
Lightning Source LLC
LaVergne TN
LVHW091636070526
838199LV00044B/1088